Workbook

WORLD ENGLISH 3

THIRD EDITION

Real People • Real Places • Real Language

Workbook

WORLD ENGLISH 3

THIRD EDITION

Real People • Real Places • Real Language

Australia • Brazil • Mexico • Singapore • United Kingdom • United States

NATIONAL GEOGRAPHIC
L E A R N I N G

National Geographic Learning,
a Cengage Company

World English Level 3 Workbook: Real People,
Real Places, Real Language, Third Edition

Publisher: Sherrise Roehr

Executive Editor: Sarah Kenney

Senior Development Editor: Lewis Thompson

Media Researcher: Leila Hishmeh

Senior Technology Product Manager:
  Lauren Krolick

Director of Global Marketing: Ian Martin

Senior Product Marketing Manager:
  Caitlin Thomas

Heads of Regional Marketing:
  Charlotte Ellis (Europe, Middle East and Africa)
  Kiel Hamm (Asia)
  Irina Pereyra (Latin America)

Production Manager: Daisy Sosa

Manufacturing Planner: Mary Beth Hennebury

Art Director: Brenda Carmichael

Operations Support: Hayley Chwazik-Gee

Compositor: MPS Limited

For permission to use material from this text or product,
submit all requests online at **cengage.com/permissions**
Further permissions questions can be emailed to
permissionrequest@cengage.com

World English 3 Workbook ISBN: 978-0-357-11372-1

National Geographic Learning
200 Pier Four Boulevard
Boston, MA 02210
USA

Locate your local office at **international.cengage.com/region**

Visit our corporate website at **www.cengage.com**

Printed in the United States of America
Print Number: 10   Print Year: 2024

Contents

Student's Book Scope and Sequence

Unit	Unit Goals	Grammar	Vocabulary

1 Where We Live Page 2	• Talk about How Long or How Often
	• Discuss Why People Move
	• Give Reasons and Explain Results
	• Discuss Improving Communities
	• Describe Places to Live
		Present Perfect
		  She has moved three times in her life.
		  It's been raining all day.
		So ... that
		  It's **so** dry here **that** we had to move.
			Migration
			Where You're from

2 The Mind's Eye Page 16	• Express Degrees of Liking
	• Discuss Mental Influences
	• Talk about Personal Characteristics
	• Discuss Improving Your Memory
	• Describe an Emotional Experience
		Infinitives and *-ing* Forms 1
		  He **loves to eat** chocolate.
		  We **enjoy staying** here each year.
		Using *Could*, *May*, and *Might*
		  Ed isn't here. He **might** be sick.
			Cognitive Milestones
			Personality Characteristics

3 Changing Planet Page 30	• Discuss Pollution
	• Discuss Causes and Effects
	• Discuss Animal Populations
	• Consider the Effects of Climate Change
	• Summarize Your Ideas
		The Passive 1
		  Pollution **is caused** by vehicles.
		The Past Perfect
		  By the time sea level **had risen** ten feet...
			Pollution
			Large Numbers

4 The Good Life Page 44	• Talk about the Things You Value
	• Discuss Important People or Events
	• Discuss Good Financial Habits
	• Talk about Great Jobs
	• Express Agreement or Disagreement
		Infinitives and *-ing* Forms 2
		  Finding out / To find out the information is important.
		The Passive 2
		  He**'s given** money every week.
		  He **was being given** the money yesterday.
			Things You Value
			Expressions Related to Money

5 Survival Page 58	• Say How Things Could Be Different
	• Discuss the Survival of Species
	• Talk about Threats to Survival
	• Discuss Rescues
	• Give Advice about Difficult Situations
		Unreal Conditionals
		  Dinosaurs are extinct, but if the comet **had missed**, they **might have survived**.
		Using *Wish* and *Hope*
		  I wish (that) earthquakes **didn't happen**.
		  I hope (that) we **get** no more earthquakes this year.
			Conditions of Species
			Natural Disasters

6 Art Matters Page 72	• Report Other People's Ideas
	• Express Opinions about Public Art
	• Talk about Types of Art
	• Discuss the Value of Art
	• Produce a Biographical Profile
		Reported Speech
		  Sara said **(that) she was going** to the gallery **the next day**.
		Adjective Clauses 1
		  The **architect who / that created the building** just won an award.
			Art
			Types of Art

Listening	Speaking and Pronunciation	Reading	Writing	Video Journal
Focused Listening A Discussion: Migration Factors	Discussing Reasons for Staying or Moving Describing an Ideal Place to Live Contractions with Auxiliary Verbs	Quality of Life	Writing a Paragraph Describing a City	**The World's Biggest Melting Pot** In this National Geographic video, we learn about the benefits of living in a multicultural city.
Listening for General Understanding and Specific Information An Interview: Cognitive Biases	Discussing Mental Influences Describing Emotions *Th* Sounds	How Memories are Made	Writing about an Emotional Experience	**Can You Really Tell If a Kid Is Lying?** In this TED Talk, Kang Lee explains the effect of telling lies in children.
General and Focused Listening An Interview: Extreme Weather Events	Discussing Cause and Effect Talking about Slogans Linking Words Together	Is Coffee in Danger?	Writing a Summary of Your Ideas	**Tales of Ice-bound Wonderlands** In this TED Talk, Paul Nicklen explains how a changing ecosystem can hurt the animals that live there.
General and Focused Listening A Conversation: Life-Changing Moments	Discussing Important People or Events Expressing Agreement and Disagreement Saying *To*	Want a Better Job? Work for a Better Company	Writing an Opinion Paragraph	**A Life Lesson from a Volunteer Firefighter** In this TED Talk, Mark Bezos describes how every act of generosity matters.
General and Focused Listening A Talk: Types of Fossils	Talking about the Survival of Species Giving Advice about Difficult Situations Emphasis to Express Meaning	A Birthday to Remember	Writing a Paragraph Giving Advice	**Three Things I Learned While My Plane Crashed** In this TED Talk, Ric Elias explains how your life can be changed by an event.
Listening for General Understanding A Radio Call-in Show: Public Art	Discussing Opinions about Art Talking about Profiles of Artists Thought Groups	The Art Bubble	Writing a Biographical Profile	**Antarctica: While You Were Sleeping** In this National Geographic Short Film Showcase video, Joseph Michael describes how art can raise awareness of issues related to Antarctica.

Listening	Speaking and Pronunciation	Reading	Writing	Video Journal
Focused Listening An Interview: Self-Driving Vehicles	Talking about Transportation Discussing Reviews Reduced Auxiliaries *Are* and *Have*	The Future of "Travel"?	Writing a Review	**SpaceX's Plan to Fly You across the Globe in 60 Minutes** In this TED Talk, Gwynne Shotwell explains why space travel, as a way to travel around the world, is possible.
Listening for General Understanding and Specific Information A Radio Interview: Running a Marathon	Discussing Competition Comparing and Contrasting Two Topics Intonation and Emphasis to Express Attitude	When Losing Means Winning	Writing a Compare and Contrast Text	**What I Learned When I Conquered the World's Toughest Triathlon** In this TED Talk, Minda Dentler describes the personal challenges of a triathlon competition.
Focused and General Listening A Radio Interview: The Job of a Stunt Person	Talking about Dangerous Jobs Giving Clear Instructions Consonant Clusters	Is Too Much Safety a Risk?	Writing Clear Instructions	**An Everyday Danger** In this National Geographic video, we learn about the difficulties of living with allergies.
Listening for General Understanding A Conversation: Discussing Historical Figures	Talking about Studying the Past Describing Mysterious Objects Intonation for Lists	Back to the Moon?	Writing a Description	**From Ancient to Modern** In this National Geographic video, we learn how ancient cultures have influenced our contemporary culture.
Listening for General Understanding A Talk: Research into the Experience of Learning	Talking about Learning Describing Problems and Solutions Enunciation	Games: More Than Just Fun	Writing an Email Giving Suggestions	**Sola Power** In this National Geographic video, Shabana Basij-Rasikh explains the importance of education for girls.
General and Focused Listening A Podcast: Competition and Innovation	Talking about Positive Outcomes Discussing Purposes and Results Stress in Compound Nouns	Daily Habits of Successful Innovators	Writing about Purpose and Results	**Why You Should Make Useless Things** In this TED Talk, Simone Giertz describes how playing and asking questions can lead to innovation.

Credits

Where We Live

Lesson A Vocabulary and Grammar

A Complete the sentences with the words in the box. Two words require a different form.

factor	neighborhood	population	quality of life	resident	trash

1. This is the largest city in the country, with a _____ of over one million.
2. Before you make a decision, consider all the different _____, including the price.
3. When there are problems in the building, the _____ meet and discuss what to do.
4. Unfortunately, there aren't many green spaces in this _____.
5. We moved here looking for a better _____, with less air and noise pollution.
6. I'm concerned by the amount of _____ we're producing. We don't need all that plastic.

B Match the sentence halves.

_____ **1.** These apartment buildings have shared community spaces
_____ **2.** You know there are social problems
_____ **3.** There was a multicultural festival
_____ **4.** This is a quiet residential area
_____ **5.** They live in a lively community

a. with lots of parks and not a lot of traffic.
b. where neighbors come from different cultures.
c. when there's a lot of trash in the streets.
d. with music from the immigrant communities.
e. where the residents' children can play.

C Complete each sentence with the present perfect or present perfect continuous form of the verb in parentheses.

1. I _____ never _____. (move)
2. Joshua _____ for a job since June. (look)
3. We _____ English for two years. (study)
4. Salma _____ Canada twice. (visit)
5. Alex _____ in Europe since June. (travel)
6. I _____ already _____ my homework. (finish)

D Check the sentences in which you can also use the present perfect continuous.

☐ **1.** I've been here since five o'clock.
☐ **2.** She's played tennis since she was little.
☐ **3.** They've worked on that project all week.
☐ **4.** I've always known you could do this!
☐ **5.** He's stopped drinking coffee for the month.
☐ **6.** Have you used my laptop?

▲ Many new apartment buildings have places for residents' children to play.

A Look at the photo and use the words in the box to write three sentences to describe it.

community	culture
economy	environment
migration	neighborhood
population	quality of life
relationships	resident
society	trash

◄ At the start of the 1900s, the North End neighborhood of Boston became known as "Little Italy" as the number of Italian immigrants grew.

1. _____

2. _____

3. _____

B 🎧 2 Listen. Then read the sentences and write T (true), F (false), or DS (doesn't say).

_____ 1. Grace and her husband moved to the city to experience a new culture.

_____ 2. Grace worked in a school.

_____ 3. Fatima was about 24 when she met Grace.

_____ 4. Grace was an excellent cook.

_____ 5. Grace and Fatima have been friends for more than 50 years.

_____ 6. Grace and Fatima's friendship started with a lie.

C 🎧 2 Listen again. Then complete each sentence with one word.

1. _____ factors were the main reason why Grace and her husband moved to the city.

2. When they first arrived, Grace had no _____ outside her family.

3. People in the neighborhood had different _____ backgrounds.

4. Fatima's English has _____ since she met Grace for the first time.

5. Fatima and Grace have _____ each other for a long time.

6. Grace didn't really _____ sugar.

Lesson C Vocabulary and Grammar

A Write each second sentence so that it means the same as the first. Use the word given and 1–3 more words.

1. I'm Mexican. (from)
   I'm _____ from Mexico _____ .

2. My mother is Brazilian, and my father is Irish. (half)
   I'm _____, _____ Irish.

3. My family is very large. (come)
   I _____ large family.

4. I'm Indian. (born)
   I _____ India.

5. I'm not a resident of this neighborhood. (live)
   I _____ this neighborhood.

6. I'm Vietnamese. (come)
   I _____ Vietnam.

7. I'm a New Yorker. (from)
   I'm _____ .

B Match the adjectives to the countries.

_____ 1. Caribbean	**a.** China, Japan, Vietnam
_____ 2. European	**b.** Egypt, Kenya, Morocco
_____ 3. Latin American	**c.** Cuba, Dominican Republic, Jamaica
_____ 4. Asian	**d.** France, Italy, United Kingdom
_____ 5. Middle Eastern	**e.** Finland, Norway, Sweden
_____ 6. African	**f.** Brazil, Cuba, Mexico
_____ 7. Scandinavian	**g.** Czech Republic, Hungary, Poland
_____ 8. Eastern European	**h.** Jordan, Lebanon, Saudi Arabia

C Complete the sentences with *so, so many / few*, or *so little / much*.

1. We had _____ fun that we didn't want to leave.

2. Jim was _____ tired that he fell asleep on the train and missed his stop.

3. They sold _____ tickets that they had to cancel the show.

4. He was _____ embarrassed that he couldn't say a word.

5. She has won _____ prizes that she has had to put some in a box.

6. We've had _____ rain this year that the back yard is all brown.

Australia, the International Nation

(a) _____ Over a quarter of the people who live in Australia were born in another country: about 6.7 million people out of a total population of around 25 million. More than 40 percent of Australians have at least one parent who was born in another country.

(b) _____ A little more than 200 years ago, Australia was inhabited by about 350,000 native people of many different cultural groups. Then, in 1770, the explorer James Cook sailed along the coast and brought back information about the "new" land to England. Soon after this, Australia became part of Great Britain. In 1787, the British government started sending criminals and poor people to Australia. Later, free **settlers** came to Australia to start farms. In 1850, **gold** was discovered there, so more and more people came from Europe and China hoping to get rich. Most of them never returned home, so the population began to grow.

(c) _____ In the 1940s, the government decided that the best way to develop the country was to invite more settlers to come from Europe. To attract immigrants, they offered money and other forms of help. More than one million people from Britain moved to Australia, along with several hundred thousand Europeans who had lost their homes in the Second World War.

(d) _____ In 2017, more than 262,000 people went to Australia to stay permanently. Four main types of people settle there: Some go there because employment and business opportunities are better than in their home country. Others are the children, parents, or other relatives of immigrants who have already become Australian **citizens** themselves. A third group is refugees who are escaping war or political problems in their home countries. Finally, there is a small number of Australians who previously migrated to another country and now want to come home.

(e) At the same time, Australia also sends immigrants to other countries—a smaller number. Each year, about 60,000 Australians go to live permanently in other countries. With people from so many cultures migrating in and out, Australia is truly a diverse nation.

settlers people who move to live in a new country or area, usually the first to do so
gold an expensive metal commonly used to make jewelry
citizens people who have become legal members of a country

The Sydney Opera House in Sydney, Australia, offers a mix of different art forms to appeal to the diversity of Australians.

A Read the article. Then match the sentences to paragraphs (a–d).

1. In a sense, nearly all Australians are immigrants.

2. Migration is still growing.

3. Australia has a huge amount of land.

4. Australia is one of the most multicultural countries.

B Circle the correct answers.

1. The main idea of the article is that _____.

  a. migration is very important in Australia

  b. Australia still needs more people

  c. the first immigrants to Australia came from Britain

2. The first people from outside Australia arrived in _____.

  a. 1770

  b. 1787

  c. 1850

3. The article talks about _____.

  a. people who migrate to Australia

  b. people who migrate from Australia

  c. both **a** and **b**

4. According to the article, about _____ Australians originally came from another country.

  a. 40 percent of

  b. 350,000

  c. 6.7 million

C Read the article again and complete the table in your notebook.

People who had a choice	People who had no choice	People who didn't migrate

D Complete the text with one word in each space.

There are so (1) _____ people living in Australia who were not born there that Australia is one of the most diverse countries in the world. The arrival of people from other countries started a little more than 200 years ago. At the time, about 350,000 (2) _____ people lived there. Australia became part of Great Britain. In 1787, the British started sending people who were not welcome in their country, such as criminals and poor people, to Australia. Immigration started later, first when settlers went there to farm, and then after gold was found there in 1850.

In the 1940s, the government felt that the country was so big, and had so (3) _____ people to develop it, (4) _____ it decided to attract immigrants with money or other types of help. People went, and are still going. The reasons (5) _____ been the same since then: People leave their homes because they think life will be better in their new country. Sometimes they want to join relatives who moved there and have become Australian citizens. The result is that, except for the grandchildren, great-grandchildren and great-great-grandchildren of those 350,000 original inhabitants, everybody else in Australia is an immigrant or the child, grandchild, or great-grandchild of (6) _____.

A Read the article about Australia in the previous lesson. Match the main ideas to the paragraphs.

____ Paragraph a **1.** There are four main reasons why people still want to move to Australia.

____ Paragraph b **2.** Migration has made Australia one of the most multicultural countries.

____ Paragraph c **3.** The migration traffic moves two ways, but not many Australians emigrate.

____ Paragraph d **4.** Immigrants moved to Australia soon after the news of its existence spread.

____ Paragraph e **5.** The government encouraged immigration to develop the country.

B Read the text. It can be divided into five paragraphs. Write the first two words of each paragraph.

Paragraph 1: _When we_ _____

Paragraph 2: _____

Paragraph 3: _____

Paragraph 4: _____

Paragraph 5: _____

When we ask why people move, we usually find that there are two main reasons. We call them *push factors* and *pull factors*. Push factors are negative: they are the reasons why people want to leave a place. Pull factors are positive: they are what attract people to a place. The majority of both of these types of factors fall into one of three groups: economic, environmental, or social factors. Economic factors are linked to money. These include the cost of living, the cost of housing, employment, or career options. A push factor could be a shortage of jobs in an area. A pull factor could be companies that offer high salaries. Pollution or, increasingly, the effect of global warming are examples of environmental factors. Long periods without rain and more frequent extreme weather are push factors. Good air quality and the presence of water are pull factors. Social factors have to do with quality of life. War, political problems, or high levels of crime are the most common push factors. Good public services, low levels of crime, and lively cultural activities are often pull factors.

C The first sentence of a paragraph introduces the main idea. Other sentences in a paragraph expand this idea. You are going to write a text of four to five paragraphs about the reasons why people leave or come to your native country. Write the first sentence for each paragraph.

Introduction: _____

_____

Paragraph 2: _____

_____

Paragraph 3: _____

_____

Paragraph 4 (optional): _____

_____

Conclusion: _____

_____

D Expand your ideas and write the text in your notebook. Write at least 150 words.

Review

A Match each word or phrase to a set of expressions.

| a lot of | be | be from | factors | high | multicultural |

1. _____ residents / trash / factors

2. a _____ community / neighborhood / society

3. _____ quality of life / level of migration / house prices

4. _____ Chinese / from Colombia / a New Yorker

5. economic / environmental / personal _____

6. _____ around here / India / Tokyo

B Circle the correct words in the paragraph.

My cousin (1) *has been moving* / *has moved* to Canada. He says there are better (2) *weather* / *employment* opportunities there and the (3) *environment* / *political* is cleaner. Canada is (4) *that* / *so* big (5) *that* / *so* there are a lot of places with small populations. My cousin (6) *has been traveling* / *was traveling* a lot since he arrived. He tries to visit somewhere new when he has free time. He is very happy in his new home. He says migration (7) *has been making* / *has made* Canada a great place to live because you meet people from a lot of different countries.

C Write complete sentences using *so*, *so many* / *few*, or *so much* / *little*, and the words given.

1. He was / emotional / started to cry.
   He was so emotional that he started to cry.

2. The website had / hits / crashed.

   _____

3. The shop had / customers / closed down.

   _____

4. I had / work to do / got home very late last night.

   _____

5. She had / help / gave up in the end.

   _____

D Complete the sentences. Use one to three words in each space.

1. Dan says he _____ a lot better since he _____ smoking.

2. We _____ from Maggie and Jim since they moved to New York.

3. My daughters _____ vegetarians since they realized it helps the environment.

4. I _____ to contact that office all day, but my call won't connect.

5. Ben _____ just _____. He said not to wait for him because he has
   so _____ work to do that he can't make it.

Video   The World's Biggest Melting Pot

A Read the sentences. Then watch the video and write *T* (true) or *F* (false). Correct the false sentences in your notebook.

_____ **1.** The narrator says that New York is a global village.

_____ **2.** The residents come from the same country and speak the same language.

_____ **3.** The speakers in the video are happy about the diversity of Queens.

_____ **4.** A woman says that in Queens there are a lot of people from Spanish-speaking countries.

_____ **5.** The same woman says that there are also a lot of people from Saudi Arabia.

B Read the sentences. Then watch the video and number the sentences in the order you hear them.

_____ **a.** So, as far as I know, we've always been Puerto Rican.

_____ **b.** But that part, I'm not sure.

_____ **c.** Who understands an immigrant better than an immigrant?

_____ **d.** Queens, New York, is a great example of a melting pot.

_____ **e.** My parents lived there, and my grandparents lived there.

___1___ **f.** Many large modern cities are very multicultural.

_____ **g.** I like that, I like that very much.

_____ **h.** They speak almost 150 different languages.

C Match the words in bold to the definitions.

_____ **1.** One neighborhood in particular **claims** to be one of the most diverse places in the world.

_____ **2.** No racial or **ethnic** group is a majority here.

_____ **3.** On my father's side, I am German, Irish, English, and I think a little bit of **Native American**.

_____ **4.** How likely is it that two **randomly selected** people have different backgrounds?

_____ **5.** How likely is it that two randomly selected people have different **backgrounds**?

_____ **6.** In their study, Queens **scored highest** in the United States.

a. the original people who lived in America before settlers arrived

b. had the most points

c. say that something is true, even if you cannot prove it

d. chosen by chance, not following a plan

e. the things that make a person the way they are: family, education, and experience

f. related to a large group of people who have the same national, racial, or cultural origins

D How diverse is the area where you live? Which are the main ethnic groups? Write a paragraph (100 words) in your notebook to describe your community.

The Mind's Eye

Lesson A Vocabulary and Grammar

A Complete the sentences with the words in the box. Three words require a different form.

> affect   belief   challenge   connect   detect   development   imagine   method

1. Creative people can _____ things that don't exist yet.

2. This was too easy. Not a _____ at all. I'm bored now.

3. She was never the same after that experience. It deeply _____ her.

4. Thank you for _____ me with her. We have so much in common.

5. What's the name of those things that _____ smoke and sound the alarm?

6. You won't be able to change his _____ in the goodness of humanity.

7. I'm sure there's a _____ to do this the right way, but I don't know it.

8. Her research has led to some amazing _____.

B Circle the correct options.

1. Would you mind *to pass* / *passing* the salt, please?

2. You agreed *to help* / *helping* me—you can't change your mind now!

3. Tell them *to avoid* / *avoiding* an argument with him at all costs.

4. I usually enjoy *to dance* / *dancing*, but I'm not feeling well right now.

5. Did she manage *to get* / *getting* there in time for her train?

6. She wants to delay *to have* / *having* the operation, but I think that's a bad idea.

C Complete the text with the correct form (infinitive or *-ing* form) of the verbs in parentheses. More than one answer may be possible.

Sardinia has become a popular tourist attraction in the last few years, so if you decide (1) _____ (visit) and you want (2) _____ (avoid) the tourist traps, this is the website for you.

If you like (3) _____ (lie) in the sun and plan (4) _____ (spend) most of your time on a beach, choose anywhere on the west coast or the east coast, south of the town of Olbia.

If you are one of those people who can't stand (5) _____ (find) sand in your shoes and don't mind (6) _____ (walk) around beautiful cities, there are other options for you. Start in the capital city, Cagliari; from there you may want (7) _____ (go) north to the prehistoric village of Barumini, and then continue (8) _____ (travel) toward the northwest to see the ruins of the Roman settlement of Tharros.

▲ Cagliari Cathedral was first built in the 13th century and overlooks the city.

A 🎧 4 Listen to the conversation. What is the relationship between the two speakers?

The speakers are _____ and _____.

B 🎧 4 Listen again. Circle the correct options.

1. Jane is reading a book
   a. as homework.
   b. after seeing a TV show.
   c. because her dad asked her to.

2. Sherlock Holmes
   a. is a police officer.
   b. is a police detective.
   c. helps the police.

3. Arthur Conan Doyle is
   a. the author of the stories.
   b. the director of the TV show.
   c. a doctor.

4. Sherlock Holmes
   a. was born in 1891.
   b. died in 1891.
   c. is completely fictional.

▲ Sherlock Holmes is often shown wearing a hunting cap.

C Read the sentences and write *T* (true), *F* (false), or *NI* (no information).

_____ 1. Jane watched a modern version of the Sherlock Holmes stories on TV.

_____ 2. Jane's dad doesn't like the idea of the TV series.

_____ 3. Jane didn't really like the TV series because Sherlock is overconfident.

_____ 4. Sherlock is happy when the police ask him to help.

_____ 5. The author of the original Sherlock stories is Arthur Conan Doyle.

_____ 6. Sherlock uses scientific methods and observation to solve difficult cases.

_____ 7. Jane's dad can't understand why she likes detective stories.

_____ 8. Jane is not surprised that her dad likes detective stories.

D Complete the paragraph with the correct form of the verbs in the box. When two answers are possible, write both.

| enjoy | go | read | read | see | suggest | visit | watch | watch |

Jane decided (1) _____ the book because she enjoyed (2) _____ the TV show. She hasn't finished (3) _____ the book, so she doesn't know which she likes best, the book or the TV version. Her father didn't know she liked (4) _____ detective shows. He, on the other hand, is a big fan of these novels, so he hopes (5) _____ Jane become a fan, too. He has always wanted (6) _____ Sherlock Holmes' house at 221B Baker Street in London, England. Of course, her father knows that Sherlock never lived there, because Sherlock is the product of Conan Doyle's imagination, but the idea of visiting the house of an imaginary man is so much fun that he hopes Jane will agree (7) _____ with him. If Jane keeps (8) _____ Sherlock's stories, he's planning (9) _____ the trip for next summer.

Lesson C Vocabulary and Grammar

A Complete each sentence with a word from the box.

| anxious | cheerful | easygoing | outgoing | reliable | selfish | sensible | shy |

1. Do you think it's easy to talk to strangers if you're as _____ as I am? I'm terrified.

2. Sue is really _____. She's always calm and never panics.

3. Everything will be fine. There's no need to be so _____. It's all under control.

4. Omar has lots of friends because he's very sociable and _____.

5. I was feeling down, but you're always so _____ that I feel a lot more positive now.

6. I don't like him. He's very _____. He only takes and never gives.

7. If you need advice, talk to Magda. She's very _____.

8. Beto is the most _____ person I know. If he says he'll do something, he will do it.

B Read the sentences. Write *U* if the modal shows uncertainty about something being true or *P* if it shows possibility about something now or in the future.

_____ 1. I think the show is on Thursday, but it might be on Friday.

_____ 2. If the pizza place is full, we could always go to the Mexican restaurant.

_____ 3. His name might be Alex—ask Lucia. She's in his class.

_____ 4. If I get a taxi now, I could be there in ten minutes.

_____ 5. He might be 18 or 20 years old.

_____ 6. If they need help, they could ask Tom. He knows everything.

_____ 7. Why don't we go to India? We could fly to Bangalore from here.

_____ 8. She might be Canadian. She's definitely not from the US.

C Rewrite the sentences using *could*, *may*, or *might* so that they mean the same.

1. There is a possibility that they will not be able to come.
   They may not be able to come.

2. I'm not sure I've met him before.

3. We are thinking of going to Rio de Janeiro this summer.

4. Perhaps she'll apply for that job.

5. I didn't study hard enough, and it is possible I will fail the exam.

6. I think she's Betty's sister.

7. He's probably 70 years old.

Norman Cousins was a famous American magazine editor. In 1964, he returned from an overseas trip and became very sick. He was in terrible pain and couldn't move his body, so he went to a hospital. Doctors told him he had a serious disease called *ankylosing spondylitis*. As nobody knew the cause of the disease, there was no **cure** for it, and because there was no cure, the doctors said he had only a short time to live. (a) _____

Cousins researched the connection between emotions and chemical reactions in the body. He believed that negative emotions could **harm** your health and that positive emotions were the key to good health, so he decided to try an experiment: he was going to fill his days with good feelings and laughter and see if that might improve his condition.

He left the hospital and moved into a hotel room. There, he got a large supply of comedy TV shows, movies, and cartoons. (b) _____ He planned to spend the whole day laughing and thinking about happy things.

On his first night in the hotel, for the first time in weeks, Cousins slept comfortably for a few hours. This seemed to prove his belief was correct: laughing at the movies might have helped his body produce chemicals that reduced pain, and as a result, he was able to rest, and his condition improved. Every time the pain came back, he watched another funny movie and laughed until he felt better.

Over time, Cousins managed to measure changes in his body with blood tests. He found that the harmful chemicals in his body decreased at least five percent every time he watched a funny movie. Therefore, after a short time, he was able to stop taking all of his medications. (c) _____

Cousins later wrote a book about how laughter and happiness helped him survive a deadly illness. As the idea of an emotional cure for a physical illness was so new, many people didn't believe his story. Many said that his doctors were wrong about his disease from the beginning. But since then, research has found that emotions affect physical health. Now everybody knows that we can become ill after long periods of stress because stress reduces our defenses. (d) _____ And Norman Cousins lived another 26 years after he cured himself from an incurable disease.

cure something that makes you healthy again
harm cause injury or hurt

A-maze-ing Laughter is a bronze sculpture by Yue Minjun. The Chinese artist hopes that the art inspires laughter and playfulness in everyone who sees it.

A Skim the article about Norman Cousins and check the best title.

☐ **1.** Medicines Can be Useless

☐ **2.** The Mind-Body Connection

☐ **3.** Movies are Good for You

▲ Norman Cousins

B Read the article. Four sentences are missing. Match the sentences to the spaces.

1. Finally, his condition improved so much that he could go back to work.

2. More experiments found that laughter can help to reduce pain.

3. They gave him powerful drugs, but his condition only got worse.

4. He also hired a nurse to read funny stories to him.

C Read the sentences and circle *T* (true), *F* (false), or *NI* (no information).

1.	Norman Cousins got sick while he was traveling in another country.	T	F	NI
2.	Doctors told Cousins that he would probably die from his disease.	T	F	NI
3.	Drugs helped to stop the pain of Cousins' disease.	T	F	NI
4.	Cousins started watching movies because he was bored.	T	F	NI
5.	Cousins spent a lot of time laughing every day.	T	F	NI
6.	Movies were better than funny stories for stopping pain.	T	F	NI

D Read the article again. Then complete the table with causes and effects.

Cause	Effect
Cousins was in terrible pain and couldn't move his body,	*so he went to a hospital.*
As nobody knew the cause of the disease,	there was no cure for it.
Because there was no cure,	
	so he decided to try an experiment.
Laughing at the movies might have helped his body produce chemicals that reduced pain.	
	Therefore, after a short time, he was able to stop taking all of his medications.
As the idea of an emotional cure for a physical illness was so new,	

Lesson E Writing

A Read the blog post about a TV movie. Then match the sentence halves.

Gina's Movies and Books

I have recently been reading Agatha Christie's novels about detective Hercule Poirot because I saw a TV version of one of her most popular books: *The A. B. C. Murders.*

It's a cool story: There's a police officer who doesn't like Poirot, but we know Poirot is the good guy, so we don't trust the officer. However, as the officer says Poirot is not who he says he is, and Poirot does not defend himself, we don't know what to think. Also, Poirot keeps seeing mental images of something terrible that might be from his own past. As a result, everything seems even more uncertain.

Then there's a young man who seems crazy and, given that he is always near the scenes of the murders, this makes us think he's the killer. A young woman, who seems like a good person, is in love with him; therefore, it seems like she may be in danger.

In the end, nothing is what it seemed. Poirot solves the case and we discover his terrible, painful secret. After a show like that, you just *have* to read the book, right?

_____ **1.** Gina has been reading Christie novels   **a.** because she enjoyed a TV show.

_____ **2.** She didn't like the police inspector   **b.** because Poirot is hiding something.

_____ **3.** She didn't know what to think   **c.** because he attacks Poirot.

_____ **4.** Poirot is sad   **d.** because he has painful memories.

B Read the blog post again. Underline the words or phrases that show cause and circle the ones that show effect.

C Rewrite the sentences. Write one leading with the cause and one leading with the effect.

1. He had no experience in the field. He didn't get the job.

    a. _Given that he had no experience in the field, he didn't get the job._

    b. _He had no experience in the field, and as a result, he didn't get the job._

2. The Governor decided to resign. He called a press conference.

    a. _____

    b. _____

3. She had to get up at four o'clock this morning. She needs to sleep.

    a. _____

    b. _____

4. You are not going out. Can I borrow your car?

    a. _____

    b. _____

5. His job is very stressful. He's very tired.

    a. _____

    b. _____

D In your notebook, write a 100-word paragraph about a difficult situation, showing at least two causes and two effects.

Review

A Write numbers to put the conversation in the best order.

___1___ **a.** Do you know anything about dyslexia?

_____ **b.** Well, it's a challenge, but there are methods. Dyslexia doesn't affect intelligence.

_____ **c.** My brother's teacher noticed he can't see letters in the right order, so he did a test.

_____ **d.** It doesn't?

_____ **e.** How do you detect it?

_____ **f.** Yes. My brother has it. It affects your ability to read and write.

_____ **g.** Wow. How can you learn if you can't read?

_____ **h.** No. People with dyslexia have strong visual, creative, and problem-solving skills.

B Complete the text with words about personality characteristics. The first letters are given.

Are you an (1) a_____ person or are you (2) e_____? I think I can be both. It

depends on the situation. Sometimes I'm really (3) s_____, and I hate being with people I don't

know, and sometimes, when I'm feeling positive, I'm (4) c_____ and (5) o_____.

It's strange when you think that I want to work in public relations. Do you think that's not a (6) s_____

idea? You may be right. In that type of work, you need to be able to manage your feelings a bit better—

you need to be (7) r_____. You can't just say, "Well, that's the way I'm feeling, and that's that."

That would be (8) s_____, right?

C Complete the sentences with the correct form of the verbs in the box. If two forms are possible, write both.

1. I'm sorry, I haven't managed _____ to Ahmed about it yet.

2. The government is planning _____ a new library here.

3. I hate _____ in this weather—I can't see anything!

4. Can I borrow that book when you finish _____ it?

5. Dad promised _____ us to Los Angeles this spring.

6. Ask Pedro. He doesn't mind _____ personal questions.

| answer |
| build |
| drive |
| read |
| take |
| talk |

D Complete the sentences using the verbs in the box and a modal.

1. He _____ the greatest musician of all time.

2. She _____ if she plays well.

3. We _____ there in an hour or two.

4. I _____ to that island. I don't think it's too far.

5. Ben _____ tonight, if he has any news.

| be |
| call |
| get |
| swim |
| win |

A Read the sentences. Then watch the first part of the video and write *T* (true), *F* (false), or *NI* (no information). Correct the false sentences in your notebook.

_____ **1.** Johnny told someone he was his father.

_____ **2.** A *poor liar* is someone who tells lies because they have no money.

_____ **3.** Children lie when they think they can.

_____ **4.** If you detect a lie, you know that someone is lying.

_____ **5.** If you have a character flaw, your personality is not perfect.

_____ **6.** A pathological liar cannot avoid telling lies.

_____ **7.** Research shows that all children are pathological liars.

_____ **8.** Research shows that girls lie more often than boys.

B Complete the sentences with the terms in the box.

> child-protection lawyer   customs officer   judge   law school student
>
> police officer   social worker   undergraduate

1. A(n) _____ is a member of the police force.

2. A(n) _____ works to protect children's rights.

3. A(n) _____ is a university student who hasn't graduated yet.

4. A(n) _____ checks that people and goods enter or leave a country legally.

5. A(n) _____ works to provide help to people who need it.

6. A(n) _____ studies law at college.

7. If a jury decides that a person is guilty, the _____ decides how to punish that person.

C Complete the table with the terms in the previous exercise. Terms can only be used once.

Experience with children	Experience with liars	No experience with children
_____	_____	_____
_____	_____	_____
_____	_____	_____

D Write about a time when it may not be bad to lie. Write about 100 words in your notebook.

Changing Planet

Lesson A Vocabulary and Grammar

A Complete the sentences with the words in the box. One word requires a different form.

| created | effects | experienced | law | level | negative | pollution | quality | thick | vehicles |

1. They printed the photos on very high-_____ paper.
2. The government passed a _____ against industries that pollute.
3. The research reveals dangerous _____ of plastics in the ocean.
4. The negative _____ of her actions surprised Jane.
5. The new public transport system reduced the number of _____ on our streets.
6. The _____ answer disappointed us.
7. _____ causes serious health problems.
8. _____ fog makes driving very dangerous.
9. The energy company _____ thousands of new jobs.
10. They _____ something new and exciting.

B Rewrite the sentences in the passive. Use the same verb form.

1. A famous professor wrote that book.
   That book was written by a famous professor.

2. Bees make honey.
   _____

3. The science teachers select the best biology project in the school.
   _____

4. The police found the lost children.
   _____

5. The government built many new schools.
   _____

6. *National Geographic* publishes all of his conservation articles.
   _____

7. Scientists didn't conduct the experiment.
   _____

C In your notebook, rewrite the completed sentences from **A** in the passive.

Lesson B Listening

A 🎧 6   Listen to the conversation. Circle the correct options to describe the speakers' project.

Miguel and Shaniqua are making a *quote* / *video* about the effects of *nature* / *pollution*.

B 🎧 6   Listen again and write *T* (true), *F* (false), or *DS* (doesn't say). Correct the false sentences in your notebook.

_____ **1.** Miguel found something he and Shaniqua can use for their project.

_____ **2.** Greenpeace used the exact words somebody else said.

_____ **3.** The article gives the name of the person who said the words.

_____ **4.** Shaniqua agrees they should change the words.

_____ **5.** Miguel has a store.

_____ **6.** Miguel is from Bolivia.

_____ **7.** There are a lot of rivers in Bolivia.

_____ **8.** Miguel and Shaniqua agree on the message they want in their project.

C 🎧 6   Match the words to the definitions. Then listen again and check your answers.

_____ **1.** chemical   **a.** something that may kill you if you breathe, eat, or drink it

_____ **2.** destroy   **b.** the exact words that someone has said or written

_____ **3.** organization   **c.** something produced in factories or laboratories

_____ **4.** poison   **d.** damage something so much that it cannot be used or repaired

_____ **5.** profit   **e.** a group of people who work together for a specific purpose

_____ **6.** quote   **f.** the price of something minus the money it cost to produce it

D 🎧 6   Listen again and complete the quote.

"When the last (1) _____ is (2) _____, when the last (3) _____ has been

(4) _____, when the last (5) _____ has been (6) _____, then we will find out

that we (7) _____ eat (8) _____."

E   What do you think about the quote? Do you think that what it says is true? Write a paragraph (100 words) to explain your thoughts.

Oil palm trees are often cut down for the production of palm oil; however, the destruction of forests is causing an environmental disaster.

Lesson C Vocabulary and Grammar

A Write each number in words.

1. 2,047 _____

2. 50,000,000 _____

3. 78,000 _____

4. 731,000 _____

5. 115,200 _____

6. 4,650,001 _____

B Complete the paragraphs with the correct form of the words and phrases in the box. Four words and phrases do not need to change.

> damage   extreme weather events   heatwave   hit
>
> often / kill   snowstorm   tornado   usually / cause

There are two types of (1) _____: the ones that happen when they are not expected—for example, out of season—and the ones that happen in season but are much more intense than normal. A lot of damage (2) _____ by both types.

An example of the first type is a (3) _____ in spring. The white stuff can be beautiful to look at, but growing plants (4) _____ by it. Furthermore, the sudden drop in temperature affects insects and flowers in fruit trees, which may freeze and die.

Other types of extreme weather can be dangerous in any season. For example, elderly people (5) _____ during a (6) _____. The high temperatures can also start wildfires that destroy people's homes and land. Also, when an area (7) _____ by a (8) _____, the strong wind damages everything in its path.

C Rewrite the sentences using the past perfect and the words given so that they mean the same.

1. I spoke to Pavel. Then I met Angham. (when, already)
   <u>When I met Angham, I had already spoken to Pavel.</u>

2. The party started. Then Jim and Pablo arrived. (by the time, already)
   _____

3. Khalid never liked Stefan, but then they had a long talk. (until)
   _____

4. I saw that movie. I didn't want to see it. (because, before)
   _____

5. Fatima always hated math. Then she found a great teacher. (until)
   _____

6. Everything happened. We got there. (by the time, already)
   _____

What Can One City Do?

In 2008, Naema Omar decided to improve her 80-year-old house in Cambridge, Massachusetts in the United States, and make it **energy-efficient**. Firstly, to keep the heat inside in the winter, she filled the space inside the walls with **insulation**. This is usually made from chemicals, but in her house, she used something new—insulation made from recycled blue jeans and other clothes. Secondly, she replaced the windows. And lastly, she put in energy-efficient LED **lightbulbs** that use only a tiny amount of electricity. They also last 50 times longer than traditional lightbulbs.

Naema was able to do this because the Cambridge City Council had created the Cambridge Energy Alliance (CEA) the year before to encourage energy efficiency and solar power. CEA's goal was to help residents and businesses save money and reduce the city's carbon **emissions**.

The city council had started to work on reducing global warming as early as 1999. In May that year, it had voted to join Cities for Climate Protection, an international group of communities that work to reduce environmental damage from fossil fuels.

First, the council needed to study the situation. So, surveys and research were conducted, and they showed that more than 80 percent of the **carbon dioxide** produced in Cambridge was coming from buildings—not from cars.

Next, it decided to make the buildings energy-efficient. In addition to saving energy and reducing emissions, the objective was to create new jobs for local people: workers were needed to put in insulation, install energy-efficient doors and windows, and make other energy improvements on buildings.

Soon after that, however, the city council realized that eco-friendly insulation and lighting are much more expensive than the usual kind, and many people in Cambridge couldn't afford them. That's why it created the CEA and encouraged every resident and business to contact them. And that's what Naema did.

First of all, individuals or businesses can ask the CEA, which, since 2011 has been part of the city's Community Development Department, to come and look at their house or office building. Then the CEA makes a plan to save 15 to 30 percent on heating, gas, water, and electricity. Finally, it helps people take out a loan to pay for the improvements. The money that people save by being more efficient should be enough to pay back the money they borrowed.

So, it looks like one city can do a lot, if it wants to!

energy-efficient using little energy
insulation material used in construction to keep heat inside
lightbulbs glass containers that produce light when electricity passes through them
emissions gases released into the atmosphere
carbon dioxide a gas that contributes to global warming

The design of the Cambridge Public Library makes it an energy-efficient building.

A Skim the article and check the best description of its topic.

☐ **1.** The article is about how the city of Cambridge has been helping people conserve energy.

☐ **2.** The article is about the life of 80-year-old Naema Omar, a resident of Cambridge.

☐ **3.** The article is about how Naema Omar started working for the Cambridge Energy Alliance.

B Match each group or organization to its description.

1. Cambridge City Council   **a.** a group of communities working together

2. Cambridge Energy Alliance   **b.** a group existing within a larger organization

3. Cities for Climate Protection   **c.** an organization set up to encourage energy efficiency

4. Community Development Department   **d.** a government organization responsible for a city

C Read the article again. Number the events in the correct order.

_____ **a.** Naema Omar contacted the Cambridge Energy Alliance.

_____ **b.** Cambridge City Council created the Cambridge Energy Alliance.

_____ **c.** Cambridge City Council joined Cities for Climate Protection.

_____ **d.** Cambridge City Council studied the results of research into carbon dioxide emissions in the city.

_____ **e.** Cambridge City Council decided to make the city buildings energy-efficient.

_____ **f.** The Cambridge Energy Alliance became part of the Community Development Department.

D Complete the sentences with the cause or the effect.

1. Naema Omar's house wasn't energy-efficient, so _____

_____

2. The city council decided to make buildings energy-efficient because _____

_____

3. The city council realized that people needed help to make their homes energy-efficient, so _____

_____

4. People save money by being energy-efficient, so _____

_____

E Read the article again. Find all the expressions that show sequence and write them in order.

Starting point: _____, _____, _____

Following points: _____, _____, (soon) _____, _____

Concluding point: _____, _____

A Read the text and number the paragraphs in the correct order, from the introduction to the conclusion.

The Polar Vortex

_____ **a.** Secondly, and as a result of the stratosphere becoming warmer, the polar vortex broke down and the winds became much weaker.

_____ **b.** The idea that extreme cold can be caused by a rise in temperature is confusing, but this is what happened. First, the stratosphere suddenly became warmer. This, for example, happened in December 2018.

_____ **c.** That's why in early February 2019, the US Midwest froze and Chicago was nearly as cold as the North Pole.

_____ **d.** The phrase "polar vortex" was first seen in US media in 2014, when extreme cold weather affected parts of the country. As weather experts explain, however, cold weather is not produced by the polar vortex itself but by the breaking of the polar vortex. But to understand how it breaks, we need to understand what it is.

_____ **e.** Thirdly, a month later, the extremely cold air above the North Pole was no longer contained by the weaker polar vortex, so it traveled south, toward the north of Asia, Europe, and North America.

_____ **f.** First of all, there is extremely cold air above the North Pole, but it is normally kept there by very strong winds that blow around it. These winds are called the polar vortex. It is found in the stratosphere, which is between six and 30 miles above the ground. This wind vortex is like a barrier that cannot be crossed by the cold air, so it protects places south of the North Pole. But in the winters of 2014, 2018, and 2019, something went wrong.

B Write the words, phrases, or punctuation that helped you to identify the position of each paragraph.

1. Introduction: _____

2. _____

3. _____

4. _____

5. _____

6. Conclusion: _____

C Look at the chart of words that show sequence. Then look at your answers to **E** in Lesson D and the previous exercise in this lesson and complete the chart.

Starting point	Numbering	Other following points	Concluding point
first of all	firstly		

D Look at the stages of filmmaking. Write a short paragraph (80–100 words) describing the process. Remember to use words that show sequence.

cast actors   edit film   find / write a script   find distributors   find money   shoot film

A Complete the text with the active or passive form of the verbs in parentheses.

There isn't much for young people to do in my community. Six months ago, the students in my school

(1) _____ (get) together to discuss a solution. We (2) _____ (decide)

to ask the principal for access to the school's facilities for after-school classes, but he

(3) _____ (tell) us that there wasn't enough money to pay staff for that. Another

meeting (4) _____ (call). This time, parents (5) _____ (invite).

To our great surprise, they (6) _____ (volunteer) to supervise us using the facilities.

Also, baking classes and bicycle-repair workshops (7) _____ (set up). We

(8) _____ (interview) by the local TV station, and when an article about us

(9) _____ (publish) in the local paper, we (10) _____ (become)

famous. Now cakes (11) _____ (sell) and bicycles (12) _____ (fix)

at our school in the evenings.

B Write the numbers.

_____ **1.** four thousand (and) fifty-one

_____ **2.** Sixty-nine million four hundred (and) twelve

_____ **3.** Twenty-eight thousand three hundred and two

_____ **4.** Nine hundred thousand

_____ **5.** Four hundred (and) thirteen thousand nine hundred and one

_____ **6.** Sixty-two million seven hundred thirty thousand and forty-seven

C Complete the sentences with the simple past or past perfect.

1. Mami _had never spoken_ (never speak) English before she ____went____ (go) to New York last
summer.

2. I was late for class, and the teacher _____ (collect, already) the homework when I
_____ (come) in.

3. The children _____ (not be) hungry for dinner because they _____ (eat)
a lot of candy after school.

4. Danny _____ (hate, always) jazz until he _____ (go) to a concert
last year.

5. By the time the game _____ (start), the rain _____ (stop), so
everyone _____ (be) happy.

A Read this paragraph from Paul Nicklen's talk and make sure you understand the general meaning. Then watch the video and complete the text.

We're inundated with news all the time that the sea ice is disappearing and it's at its lowest

(1) _____. And in fact, scientists were originally saying sea ice is going to disappear in the next

(2) _____ years, then they said (3) _____ years. Now they're saying the sea ice in the

Arctic, the summertime, extent is going to be gone in the next four to ten years. And what does that

(4) _____? After a while of reading this in the news, it just becomes news. You sort of glaze over

with it. And what I'm trying to do with my work is put faces to this. And I want people to understand and

(5) _____ the concept that, if we lose ice, we stand (6) _____ lose an entire ecosystem.

B Read the sentences from the text in **A** and answer the questions.

1. We're inundated with news all the time that the sea ice is disappearing.
   a. Is the information about the sea ice a lot or a little?

   _____

   b. Does the news say that the sea is disappearing?

   _____

2. The sea ice in the Arctic, the summertime extent is going to be gone in the next four to ten years.
   a. Is there a difference between the amount of sea ice in the Arctic in summer and in winter?

   _____

   b. For how much longer is there going to be sea ice in the summer in the Arctic?

   _____

3. After a while of reading this in the news, it just becomes news. You sort of glaze over with it.
   a. Is Paul saying that the disappearance of sea ice should not be in the news?

   _____

   b. Is Paul saying that when we hear something in the news too often, we stop paying attention to it?

   _____

4. You sort of glaze over with it. And, what I'm trying to do with my work is put faces to this.
   a. Does "put faces to this" mean "show you the faces of the people who take these photos"?

   _____

   b. Is Paul trying to put faces to this so people can keep glazing over?

   _____

C Watch the video again. Imagine that the leopard seal is telling another seal about her encounter with Paul. Write the story (100–150 words) from the leopard seal's point of view. Use words showing sequence and make sure the seal explains the causes and effects of her actions.

The Good Life

Lesson A Vocabulary and Grammar

A Complete the text with the words in the box.

| access | afford | balance | career | criteria | income | opportunity | satisfaction | value | wealth |

My older brother, Dave, has a brilliant (1) _____. He works for a bank. He has a big house, quite

a lot of (2) _____, and can (3) _____ to buy really expensive stuff, but he works fourteen

hours a day, including weekends. He no longer has time to see his best friend Aziz from high school.

Aziz is an artist. He gets great (4) _____ from painting, but he has no (5) _____

because his paintings don't sell. He says that's because he has no (6) _____ to sell them and no

(7) _____ to art galleries, but I think the truth is that nobody likes them.

There must be a (8) _____ between these two extremes. Looking at Dave and Aziz, I've

realized that what I (9) _____ is not possessions or self-expression but experience, and above

all, shared experience. These need to be the main (10) _____ for the big decisions I'll have to

make soon.

B Complete the paragraph with the correct form (infinitive or -*ing* form) of the verbs in parentheses.

I hope (1) _____ (go) to Europe next year, so I'm trying (2) _____ (save) enough money.
I avoid (3) _____ (eat) out these days because I don't really need to. And I've given up
(4) _____ (go) to the movies. So far, I've saved 100,000 yen—that's about $1,000—but it's not
enough. I want (5) _____ (stay) in Europe for at least a month, so I need a lot more money. I've asked
my parents (6) _____ (let) me move back into their home, since my apartment is expensive, and they
said yes. But my expenses are so high that it's still not enough. Maybe I need (7) _____ (reduce)
the amount of money I spend on clothes, or I won't be able (8) _____ (afford) my trip to Europe.

C Circle the correct form in each sentence.

1. They agreed *to meet* / *meeting* again the following week.
2. He complained about *to pay* / *paying* too much for lunch.
3. We believe in *to solve* / *solving* problems by *to talk* / *talking*.
4. She promised *to call* / *calling* as soon as she got home.
5. He's not very good at *to listen* / *listening*.
6. I need *to ask* / *asking* you a big favor.
7. I'm sure you'll break the record if you keep on *to train* / *training* hard.
8. Do you know how *to fix* / *fixing* bicycles?

A 🎧 **8** Listen to the speakers and circle the correct answers.

1. Who are the speakers?

    a. teachers

    b. students

2. What are they doing?

    a. presenting a project

    b. planning a project

B 🎧 **8** Read the questions. Then listen again and circle the correct answers.

1. Which of these criteria was **not** mentioned by any of the students?

    a. medical care   **b.** life / work balance   **c.** safety

2. Which of these criteria was mentioned by almost all of the students?

    a. the environment   **b.** love   **c.** medical care

3. Which of these criteria was mentioned by all of the students?

    a. safety   **b.** the environment   **c.** love

4. Which of these criteria was mentioned by a few students?

    a. medical care   **b.** safety   **c.** the environment

C Read the sentences and write *T* (true) or *F* (false). Correct the false sentences in your notebook.

_____ **1.** The students read about a study on happiness.

_____ **2.** They decided to use the same criteria as the study.

_____ **3.** To carry out their research, they did a lot of reading.

_____ **4.** They think that some of their results are surprising.

_____ **5.** There is at least one thing all students agree is very important.

_____ **6.** All students admire the older generation for the choices they made.

_____ **7.** A lot of students want to make a difference for the future.

D 🎧 **8** Listen again and write a number to answer each question.

_____ **1.** How old are the students the team interviewed?

_____ **2.** How many students mentioned *love* as one of their criteria?

_____ **3.** How many students are sure they will never get what they want?

_____ **4.** How many students feel certain they will achieve what matters most to them in life?

_____ **5.** How many students are worried about violence and not feeling safe?

_____ **6.** How many students want to do something so that their children's lives will be better?

A Skim the article and circle the best description of its purpose.

1. To tell people how to make money from storytelling
2. To discourage people from borrowing money
3. To explain ways to fund projects

B Read the article again. Write the words and phrases in bold next to the definitions.

1. _____: giving a lot of information
2. _____: the situation after the last animal or plant of a certain species dies
3. _____: that makes people think something different from the truth
4. _____: the cost of money
5. _____: be allowed to apply or take part in something
6. _____: permission/ability to be the only one allowed to use something
7. _____: a plan about how something will happen
8. _____: at risk of no longer existing
9. _____: the activity of writing or telling stories
10. _____: the protection of plants and animals in natural areas

C Read the article again and check the correct answers.

1. Why is the phrase "borrow money from a bank" misleading?
   ☐ **a.** Banks don't borrow money.
   ☐ **b.** You can't just give back what you took.
   ☐ **c.** Banks give you interest.

2. Why are some people worried about borrowing?
   ☐ **a.** If they don't pay the loan back, they will be in trouble.
   ☐ **b.** They don't want to pay interest.
   ☐ **c.** Their families may not have money to lend them.

3. If you take photos for a project funded by the National Geographic Society, who can you sell them to?
   ☐ **a.** nobody
   ☐ **b.** anybody
   ☐ **c.** the National Geographic Society

4. If you get a grant for a project, what do you have to do at the end of the project?
   ☐ **a.** You have to pay back the exact amount of money you received.
   ☐ **b.** You have to qualify for the grant.
   ☐ **c.** You have to show that your work matches your plan.

D Read the third and sixth paragraphs again. Use different colors to highlight the topic sentence, the sentences that support the topic sentence, the sentences that give more information about the supporting sentences, and the conclusion.

A Read the opinion essay. Identify the function of each sentence and write the number. The first one has been done for you. Sentences can have more than one function.

Money Can't Buy Happiness—True or False? Discuss.

When people say that money can't buy happiness, they usually mean that you can be rich and also completely miserable. ^{1,5} If you feel empty, no amount of possessions you can buy will ever fill that space inside you. While, of course, money can buy you freedom from financial problems, happiness is beyond the reach of money.

I think the statement is true, but only up to a point. In some cases, money *can* buy happiness. It does so when happiness comes not from the thing you buy, but from what the thing allows you to do. A case in point is if you're somebody who loves running, then those high-quality running shoes you've been thinking of *will* buy you a certain amount of happiness (and help prevent injuries). Or, if you feel that there's a part of yourself that only comes out when you're playing a guitar, then that guitar *will* give you a lot of happiness. However, how do you feel when you're not running or not playing your guitar?

My point is that we need to ask ourselves what kind of happiness we are trying to buy. Is it the temporary excitement of owning something new? Is it the temporary freedom from feeling something else we do not want to feel? Or is it something that adds to our well-being? If it is a renewable source of joy, then in that case, money can buy some happiness.

1. topic sentence
2. sentence supporting the topic sentence
3. sentence giving more information about a supporting sentence
4. conclusion
5. introduction and definition of the topic
6. introduction of an opinion
7. explanation of an opinion
8. example to support an opinion
9. contrasting example

B Look at the opinion essay again, and at the text in Lesson D. Complete the table.

Ways to indicate contrast	Ways to indicate partial agreement	Ways to introduce examples
1. though	1.	1.
2.	2.	2.
3.		
4.		

C Look at the essay title below. Write a an opinion essay (100–150 words) opinion essay. Include reasons and examples to support your opinion.

An important change my school needs to make.

A Complete the sentences with the correct form of the words in the box.

> access   afford   balance   satisfaction   value

1. You need a more _____ diet.

2. I'm sure she can make a _____ contribution to the project.

3. This building needs to be made _____ to wheelchairs.

4. I'm _____ with my bronze medal.

5. According to a study of the cost of living, my city is the least _____.

6. I can't _____ the internet—is the router working properly?

7. I'm finding it difficult to _____ homework and basketball practice.

8. I'm afraid your application doesn't _____ all the requirements for this job.

9. Do you know what the _____ of this diamond is?

B Decide if the sentences are correct (*C*) or incorrect (*I*). Correct the incorrect sentences in your notebook.

_____ **1.** He asked Pedro to help him move the sofa.

_____ **2.** I got to where I am today by to work hard.

_____ **3.** It's too cold going outside today.

_____ **4.** I need to borrow your car getting to work.

_____ **5.** I need to get better at reading my teacher's feedback.

_____ **6.** It's difficult finding the time to exercise these days.

C Rewrite the sentences in the passive. If the agent is not needed, do not include it.

1. They're not answering phone calls.

_____

2. The Mayor will attend the ceremony.

_____

3. People donated large amounts of money to help the survivors.

_____

4. They will never repay this loan.

_____

5. The police officer was investigating the accident.

_____

6. They didn't set aside enough money for emergencies.

_____

7. They encourage people to make their homes energy-efficient.

_____

8. The local TV station interviewed her.

_____

A Watch the video. Then match the expressions with the definitions.

_____ **1.** footrace   **a.** very valuable things like jewels and gold

_____ **2.** barefoot   **b.** a running competition

_____ **3.** stunned   **c.** the amount of goods or people that a vehicle can carry

_____ **4.** jealousy   **d.** with no shoes or socks on

_____ **5.** payload   **e.** shocked and temporarily unable to react

_____ **6.** treasures   **f.** a feeling of anger because somebody has what you want

B Watch the first part of the talk. Then complete the summary with the words in the box.

be	charity	part	skilled	talking	was

Mark Bezos works for a (1) _____ called Robin Hood in New York. He is also the

assistant captain of a volunteer fire company. Because the professional firefighters are highly

(2) _____, volunteers need to arrive to a fire scene very early if they want to take

(3) _____ in the action.

The first time Bezos went to help fight a fire, he was the second volunteer to arrive, so he was

hoping to (4) _____ given something important to do. He ran to see his captain to ask what

he could do, and he found him (5) _____ to the owner of a burning house. The first

volunteer on the scene (6) _____ asked by the captain to go inside the house and save the

homeowner's dog.

C Self-irony is a way of making fun of yourself by showing the difference between who you would like to be and who you really are. Watch the talk again and complete the sentences about how Mark Bezos does it. Use one word in each space.

1. Mark describes his feeling as stronger than a normal person's in that situation when he says he was

_____ with _____.

2. He is greatly disappointed because the first firefighter is asked to save a dog while he only has to save

a pair of _____.

3. First, he describes the pair of _____ he carries as a _____.

4. Then, he describes the dog and the pair of _____ as _____ and he notices

that his receives less attention than the first firefighter's, which is another blow to his "hero image."

D Write a paragraph about yourself using self-irony. Write about 100 words.

Survival

Lesson A Vocabulary and Grammar

A Complete the sentences with the words in the box.

alive	disaster	discovery	extinct	hero
relationship	rescue	species	survive	terror

1. Bowhead whales can _____ for a long time. They can stay _____ for over 200 years.

2. The desert rat kangaroo is _____. The last of the _____ died in 1935.

3. Jane Goodall was considered a _____ when she made an important _____ in 1960.

4. There are organizations that help _____ animals after a natural _____.

5. Antelope usually run in _____ when they are chased by lions.

6. The close _____ between man and dog can be traced back thousands of years.

B Circle the correct options.

1. I *would help / would have helped* you if I *had / had had* time, but unfortunately, I don't.

2. If you *told / had told* him, he *would do / would have done* something about it. Now it's too late.

3. If he *got / had gotten* here in the next minute, he *would catch / would have caught* the train.

4. If they *saw / had seen* the movie, they *would like / would have liked* it, but they won't watch it.

5. She twisted her ankle before the race. If she *ran / had run*, she *would win / would have won*.

C Complete the conversation with the correct form of the verbs in parentheses.

Anya: What are you doing? You're always saying how terrifying climate change is, and then you buy water in a plastic bottle? If you (1) _____ (be) serious about the environment, you (2) _____ (not / do) that.

Jim: Really? Yesterday you had a steak for lunch. If you (3) _____ (tell) the truth all these years about how much you care for the environment, you (4) _____ (not / do) that.

Anya: I have been telling the truth! And yesterday was different—I didn't have a choice! It was a business lunch. If the restaurant (5) _____ (have) a vegetarian option, I (6) _____ (order) it. But it didn't, and I didn't want to look difficult in front of a client.

Jim: Well, I'm thirsty now, so I have no choice.

Anya: Are you saying that if you (7) _____ (not / drink) that water right now, you (8) _____ (die) of thirst?

Jim: No, but ...

Anya: There's a coffee shop around the corner. You can have a glass of tap water there. (9) _____ (it, kill) you if you (10) _____ (wait) five minutes, or is it too much to ask?

A 🎧 10 Listen to the conversation. Who is Marina?

She's _____.

B 🎧 10 Listen again and circle the correct options.

1. Hannah and Yusuf

    a. have just made a documentary.

    b. are making a documentary.

    c. have just watched a documentary.

2. Yusuf

    a. didn't want to watch the show.

    b. played a video game while he watched the show.

    c. is annoyed with Hannah because she insisted.

3. Hannah would like to work as

    a. a storyteller.

    b. a film and documentary maker.

    c. Marina.

4. Marina would live

    a. in pre-historic times.

    b. in modern times.

    c. forever.

C 🎧 10 Listen again. Then read the sentences and write *T* (true), *F* (false), or *NI* (no information).

_____ **1.** Yusuf liked the show, but less than Hannah did.

_____ **2.** The show was about global warming.

_____ **3.** Hannah has been thinking about a movie script.

_____ **4.** Marina's story is a true story.

_____ **5.** Hannah has thought about all the details in the movie.

_____ **6.** Marina would remember what nature was like before factories were built.

_____ **7.** Marina's story would be very depressing at the end.

_____ **8.** Modern teenagers would join Marina in her fight.

D Complete the sentences with the correct form of the verbs in the box.

| go | miss out | not find out | not insist | not stay | not watch |

Hannah and Yusuf are classmates and also neighbors, so they spend a lot of time at each other's houses. Yesterday, they were at Hannah's. If Hannah (1) _____ they watched a show about natural history, Yusuf (2) _____ home to play video games. If he (3) _____ the show, he (4) _____ on something really good. However, he stayed and watched it, and he really enjoyed it. Also, if he (5) _____, he (6) _____ how important natural history movies and documentaries are to Hannah.

Lesson C Vocabulary and Grammar

A Complete the sentences with words from the box.

| avalanches | drought | earthquakes | eruption | hurricanes | landslides | wildfires |

1. Many trees have been lost as a result of _____ caused by discarded cigarettes and electrical sparks.

2. Heavy rain can cause _____ on hills where there are no trees whose roots keep hillsides in place.

3. _____ happen when the earth breaks and moves. Sometimes this is caused by an _____ from a volcano.

4. If the ground shakes near mountains covered in snow, it can cause _____.

5. _____ are becoming more violent and destructive because they carry more rain and stronger winds.

6. Long heat waves are causing long periods of _____ and migrations of people in search of water.

B Read the sentences and think about their meaning. Write *Y* (yes), *N* (no), or *NI* (no information).

1. I wish you would stop making that noise.

   _____ **a.** Are you making that noise now?

   _____ **b.** Do I like that noise?

   _____ **c.** Would I like you to stop making that noise?

2. I hope you pass the exam.

   _____ **a.** Have you taken your exam?

   _____ **b.** Do you know the result of your exam?

   _____ **c.** Do I want you to fail your exam?

3. I wish you hadn't told him.

   _____ **a.** Can you undo what you did?

   _____ **b.** Am I happy that you did it?

   _____ **c.** Would I be happier if you hadn't done it?

4. I hope you passed your exam.

   _____ **a.** Did you take an exam?

   _____ **b.** Do you know the result of your exam?

   _____ **c.** Do I know the result of your exam?

C Write one sentence with *wish* and one with *hope* for each situation.

1. Rachel doesn't like her job.
   Rachel wishes she had a different job.
   Rachel hopes to get a different job.

2. Josh lives far from his school.

   _____

   _____

3. I made very few friends.

   _____

   _____

4. Please don't make so much noise.

   _____

   _____

Ready for Anything

Every day, there are news reports about natural disasters, like floods, earthquakes, and hurricanes in the media. With extreme weather conditions occurring more and more often, you may want to be ready for them. There are three important things you should do at home to prepare.

In general, the first thing is to stock up on emergency supplies. You should keep enough food and water for at least three days in your house. Choose food that can be stored for a long time and food that can be eaten without cooking. Canned foods, such as soup, fish, meat, and fruit are good choices. You can also store dry foods like crackers and nuts. On top of that, be sure to store food that you like, and include a few special treats like candy or cookies. In an emergency situation, it's nice to have something to cheer you up. As well as that, it is important to include any special foods that babies, small children, or elderly people in your family may need. Another thing is water: be sure to keep plenty of it. Each person needs one gallon of water per day for drinking and basic washing.

Generally speaking, emergencies can occur in every country in the world, but it's important to think about equipment you might need for the kinds of disasters that are more likely in your country. You might need blankets, very warm clothes, flashlights, or plastic bags. In other words, think about possible situations, and buy the things that would be needed to cope with them.

In addition, plan what you will do in case you need to evacuate your home. In particular, decide where you will go and actually arrange a meeting place in advance, such as a relative's home or a big public building. Also, be sure that all family members have the phone number of a contact person in another city. In short, have a plan to find your family members if you become separated.

To sum up: people don't like to think about natural disasters, but a little bit of preparation can save lives. Following these steps will help you be ready for any kind of emergency.

In the event of an evacuation because of a natural disaster, you may need to protect your home from damage.

A Skim the article and choose the correct ending for each sentence. Two sentence endings are extra.

_____ **1.** The article explains how …

_____ **2.** It provides suggestions about …

a. becoming separated from the rest of your family.

b. to be ready in case of a natural disaster.

c. having the right types of supplies and equipment.

d. to find the right types of supplies and equipment.

B Read the article again. Find words that mean the opposite of these words.

_____ **1.** everyday

_____ **2.** thrown away

_____ **3.** fresh

_____ **4.** young

_____ **5.** a little

_____ **6.** impossible

_____ **7.** stay in

_____ **8.** reunited

C Complete the sentences.

1. Canned foods are a good idea because _____.

2. Treats are good because _____.

3. Babies, children, and elderly people may need _____.

4. People need one gallon _____.

5. Other equipment depends on _____.

6. You may not be able to stay in your home, so you need _____.

D Read the article again. Complete the table of expressions that carry out the following functions.

Generalizing	Explaining/Giving details	Adding	Summarizing
In general,			

A Read the blog post. Then number the steps for successful writing in the correct order.

Top Tips for Writing Longer Texts in English

It can be difficult to write a long text in English, so I hope you find these suggestions useful.

To begin with, write a list of your main points, and make sure that they cover what you want to say or that they answer the questions in the task.

Then decide how you are going to say it. In other words, decide on the most effective order to present your points. For example, if you are describing a process or a series of events, you'll probably need to arrange them in the order they happen.

Once you have ordered your points, write the topic sentence for each one. As a general rule, readers should be able to skim a text—that is to say, read only the first sentence of each paragraph—to know what it is about. In addition, help readers find their way by using *markers*. For example, show order with words like *firstly* and *secondly*, and show cause and effect with words like *because* or *as a result*.

Next, expand the topic sentences. Clarify what you mean by giving examples, explaining in detail, and adding information.

Finally, write your introduction, presenting what you are going to talk about, and your conclusion, summing up the results of your points.

In conclusion, if you follow these steps, and you use appropriate and correct language, you can write a good text.

_____ **a.** Write the last paragraph.   _____ **d.** Write the first paragraph.

_____ **b.** Write topic sentences.   _____ **e.** Explain your points with supporting sentences.

_____ **c.** Organize the order of your content.   _____ **f.** Write your content in the form of a list.

B Look at the chart about markers and copy it into your notebook. Then complete it with the markers from the text and the markers from **D** in Lesson D.

Ordering	Generalizing	Giving details	Adding	Summarizing

C Read the information. Rewrite the text, organizing the information into paragraphs, connecting the sentences, and using appropriate markers.

Sir Ernest Henry Shackleton (1874–1922) was an Anglo-Irish polar explorer who led three British expeditions to the South Pole. On the third one, he decided to cross Antarctica from sea to sea via the South Pole. He led the expedition with a crew of 28 men on a ship called *Endurance*. The *Endurance* got trapped in ice. Shackleton and his men abandoned it. They took the lifeboats from the ship. They camped on the ice. The ice started to break, so they had to leave. They went back to sea on the lifeboats. After five days, they landed on a remote island, Elephant Island. Shackleton decided to take five men on one of the lifeboats to try to find help. They reached another island, South Georgia, after two weeks. It was the wrong side of the island: there was only one village, on the other side of it. He left three men where they had landed and crossed the island on foot. He found help. He sent a boat to rescue the three men on the other side of South Georgia. He organized an expedition to rescue the men on Elephant Island. He went on the expedition. All the men were rescued. It was a disaster, and the expedition failed, but everybody survived.

A Write each second sentence so that it means the same as the first. Use the correct form of the words given and 1–4 more words.

1. It was a terrible accident. We're lucky we didn't die. (alive)

   It was a terrible accident. We're _____.

2. We have lost many species of plants and animals because of pollution. (extinct)

   Many species of plants and animals _____ because of pollution.

3. The firefighters brought everybody out of the burning house. (rescue)

   _____ from the burning house.

4. A lot more needs to be done to ensure that the planet isn't destroyed. (survive)

   A lot more needs to be done to ensure _____ of the planet.

5. Human activity is having an extremely negative effect on nature. (disaster)

   Human activity is having _____ on nature.

6. Have you found anything interesting? (discover)

   Have you made _____?

7. Suddenly, a strange and loud noise scared everybody. (terror)

   Suddenly, there was a _____.

8. I'm sure these two events are connected. (relationship)

   I'm sure there's a _____ events.

9. A lot of people admire him because he risked his life to save strangers. (hero)

   A lot of people consider _____ he risked his life to save strangers.

10. Dogs and wolves have very similar characteristics. (species).

    Dogs and wolves are a _____.

B Complete the sentences with the correct form of the verbs in parentheses.

1. If we hadn't been in such a hurry, we _____ (remember) where we parked the car.

2. If there _____ (be) a tornado, it would destroy our town.

3. I _____ (not / stay) in this town if my family didn't need me to help them.

4. We _____ (go) on the trip if he hadn't gotten sick.

C Complete the text with the correct form of the verbs in parentheses. Sometimes more than one form is correct.

1. I hope _____ (become) a computer engineer after I leave school, so I did an

   evening course.

2. The course was expensive. I wish I _____ (choose) a cheaper one.

3. I wish I _____ (have) more patience. I took my computer apart after just one lesson.

4. I wish I _____ (not / do) that, because I didn't know how to put it back together.

5. I wish I _____ (listen) to the teacher's advice.

6. I'm looking at my computer now, and I hope I _____ (not / damage) it too seriously.

A Read these sentences from the talk. What do the words in bold refer to? Watch the talk and circle the correct answers.

1. So I looked at **them** right away, and they said, "No problem. We probably hit some birds."
   a. other passengers
   b. the flight attendants
   c. the engines

2. **That**'s usually not the route.
   a. Manhattan
   b. three things happening at the same time
   c. the Hudson River

3. **He** says, "Brace for impact."
   a. the pilot
   b. the flight attendant
   c. the person imagining a plane with no sound

4. I could see in **her** eyes, it was terror.
   a. the person called Brace
   b. the flight attendant
   c. the person who spoke

5. I learned that **it** all changes in an instant.
   a. the plane's direction
   b. the things you do
   c. the way you see everything

6. And **this** is as we clear the George Washington Bridge, which was by not a lot.
   a. the George Washington Bridge
   b. learning the second thing
   c. the urgency

7. And after, as I reflected on **that**, I decided to eliminate negative energy from my life.
   a. time wasted on things that didn't matter
   b. how good his life was
   c. time wasted trying to get better at everything

8. It's almost like we've been preparing for **it** our whole lives.
   a. being sad
   b. dying
   c. coming down fast

B Match the two halves of the sentences.

_____ 1. A route is the way you
_____ 2. If something is over,
_____ 3. A bucket list is things you
_____ 4. When you mend fences, you
_____ 5. You feel regret when you wish you
_____ 6. Someone's ego is their

a. had done something differently.
b. resolve conflicts with other people.
c. go to reach a certain place.
d. sense of self-importance.
e. want to do in the future.
f. it's finished.

C Think of a regret you have about a time you chose to be right rather than happy. Write about what you would do differently now. Write 100–150 words.

Art Matters

Lesson A Vocabulary and Grammar

A Complete the sentences with the words in the box.

> controversial   creative   display   exhibition   gallery   genius   inspire   installation   portraits   unique

1. All artists use their imaginations. They are _____.
2. Some artists challenge rules. This makes them _____, and their works _____ debate.
3. An artist who changed the rules and saw things differently is sometimes called a _____.
4. Do _____ always show someone at a specific moment in time?
5. Is a work of art a _____ piece created by the artist?
6. Marcel Duchamp put ready-made objects on _____ in an _____.
7. Is art only considered "art" because it's in an art _____?
8. _____ art can be interactive and is designed to change our feelings about the space it is in.

B Use the correct form of the words in bold and one or two other words to complete the sentences.

1. Her generosity has **inspired** all of us.

   Her generosity has been _____ for all of us.

2. Her work shows great **creativity** from an early age.

   She _____ from an early age.

3. His statements on TV were very **controversial**.

   His statements on TV caused _____.

4. They tried to **install** special lighting, but they failed.

   The _____ special lighting failed.

5. He put his award on **display** in his living room.

   He _____ award in his living room.

C Write what each person said. Use reported speech and make all the necessary changes.

1. Tomoko said, "I have a headache."

   _____

2. "I live in New York," said Rita.

   _____

3. The president said, "I have a plan to help our country."

   _____

4. "I can't go to the movies because I'm doing my homework," said Mohammed.

   _____

Lesson B Listening

A 🎧 12 Listen to the podcast about the controversy between James Whistler and John Ruskin in 1877. Check the best title for the episode.

☐ **1.** How much is that pot of paint?

☐ **2.** Painters and Fireworks

☐ **3.** The Artist and the Art Critic

B 🎧 12 Read the sentences. Then listen again and write *T* (true) or *F* (false).

_____ **1.** James Whistler exhibited a painting called *Nocturne in Black and Gold: The Falling Rocket* in a London gallery.

_____ **2.** The painting shows fireworks on the River Thames.

_____ **3.** The painting shows the area around the River Thames in great detail.

_____ **4.** John Ruskin's opinions could have disastrous effects on an artist's career.

_____ **5.** Ruskin admired Whistler as a person.

_____ **6.** Ruskin thought Whistler worked too fast.

_____ **7.** Whistler started a legal battle against Ruskin.

_____ **8.** Whistler's battle was a great success.

▲ A statue of James Whistler in London shows the artist looking out over the River Thames.

C 🎧 12 Complete the sentences with the words in the box. Then listen and check your answers.

> court   damages   legal   libel   sue

1. You _____ someone if you write that they have done something wrong and you can't prove it.

2. If somebody breaks the law in a way that damages you, you can _____ them.

3. If you take _____ action against somebody, you can win or lose.

4. If somebody loses money because of something you did, they can ask you to pay _____ to them.

5. A _____ is a place where people decide if someone did or did not break the law.

D 🎧 13 Listen and write the extracts as reported speech.

1. Carla said that Ruskin _had insulted Whistler. He had said that the painting was trash, and he had said it in a newspaper._

2. Carla asked _____.

3. Professor Connolly said that Whistler _____.

4. Carla said that Whistler _____.

5. Professor Connolly told Carla that Whistler said _____.

6. Professor Connolly said that, for Whistler, _____.

7. Carla said _____.

Lesson C — Vocabulary and Grammar

UNIT 6

A Complete the chart with the words in the box. Some words can be used more than once.

| architecture | ceramic art | design | fashion | graffiti | illustration | literature |
| media art | movies | music | painting | photography | sculpture | |

2D art	3D art	Craft art	Storytelling art	Performance art

B Complete the sentences with the correct form of words from the box in **A**. Use words only once.

1. He did a great _____ for our event poster.
2. The _____ of some birds' nests can be very complex.
3. The Great Sphinx of Giza is one of the most famous _____ in the world.
4. She has produced some controversial multi-_____ installations.
5. Do you think _____ has changed a lot since the introduction of digital cameras?
6. Dresses made by some _____ designers are considered works of art.
7. Leonardo DiCaprio is my favorite _____ star.
8. This phone has a really cool _____.

C Complete the adjective clauses with *who*, *that*, or *which*. When two answers are correct, write both.

1. Jane, this is Mira, the woman _____ helped me at the station.
2. Neil Armstrong, _____ was the first man to walk on the Moon, died in 2012.
3. The tablet _____ you are using is Pedro's.
4. The tree _____ we planted, _____ is an oak, is doing very well.
5. The twins, _____ didn't come to school today, are my best friends.
6. The movie _____ won the Oscar for best film cost very little money.
7. The painting _____ was stolen last week was a fake.
8. The young men _____ are talking to Dad are the ones _____ gave me a ride when my car, _____ is now in the shop, broke down on the highway.

The home of Frida Kahlo, which she shared with Diego Rivera, is now a museum dedicated to her life and work.

Biographies of Great Artists: Frida Kahlo

Frida Kahlo was born in Mexico in 1907. As a small child, she was very happy and ran and laughed all the time—even in church. However, when she was six years old, her life changed completely. She got a serious disease called polio and had to remain in bed for nine months. (a) _____.

In spite of this, Frida was able to lead a normal life, and at 15, she was enrolled in a prestigious school in Mexico City. There, she was influenced by the modern changes that were sweeping across Mexico. She cut her hair short like a boy and started riding a bicycle—(b) _____. She was very interested in science and decided to become a doctor.

Then, in September, 1925, Frida was involved in a horrendous accident. She was riding on a bus when it crashed into a trolley car. Her right leg was broken in 11 places, and she had many other broken bones. (c) _____.

On the one hand, this was obviously a tragedy: as well as living with pain, she also had to give up her plans to become a doctor because she knew she would never be strong enough. On the other hand, it also helped her discover something else about herself. While lying in bed after the accident, Frida began reading books about art. Her father was a painter and photographer, and he encouraged her interest in the subject. Frida was not only someone who did not give up easily, but she was also very talented. (d) _____.

In 1929, Frida married the famous Mexican artist Diego Rivera, and although she was a more original painter than he was, for a long time she was known just as Diego Rivera's wife. However, soon famous artists such as André Breton, Marcel Duchamp, and Georgia O'Keeffe noticed her and praised her work, and after an exhibition in Manhattan in 1938, she became very famous in the US, France, and Mexico. Still, she struggled to make a living from her art because (e) _____.

She continued to paint all her life, even though her health became increasingly bad. Although she was bedridden when a famous gallery organized an exhibition of her work not long before her death, she insisted on attending the opening ceremony, and her bed was carried into the gallery so that (f) _____.

Frida died in 1954, at the age of 47, but her paintings, her life, and her ideas still attract a lot of attention. In 2002, a popular movie, which was nominated for six Oscars and won two, was made of her life, with Salma Hayek as Frida, (g) _____.

A Read the article. Parts of the text are missing. Match the parts to the spaces.

_____ **1.** she could talk to visitors

_____ **2.** One year later, she completed her first painting: a portrait of herself

_____ **3.** shocking for a young woman of her time

_____ **4.** For the rest of her life, she had severe pain every day caused by that accident

_____ **5.** and she is also a character in the 2017 animated movie *Coco*

_____ **6.** The disease made her left leg shorter than her right, so she had serious problems walking

_____ **7.** she refused to adapt her style to some of her clients' requests

B Look at the words from the text and match them to the definitions.

_____ **1.** biographies

_____ **2.** remain

_____ **3.** sweeping

_____ **4.** horrendous

_____ **5.** severe

_____ **6.** encourage

a. extremely bad

b. moving very fast

c. very strong

d. stay

e. support and help

f. stories of people's lives

C Circle *T* (true) or *F* (false).

1. Frida Kahlo had a happy childhood until she was six.	T	F
2. As a teenager, Frida liked modern ideas.	T	F
3. Frida became a doctor.	T	F
4. Frida began painting after she suffered a terrible accident.	T	F
5. Frida's father and husband were artists, too.	T	F
6. Frida only became famous soon before she died.	T	F
7. Frida had to stop painting when her health became worse.	T	F
8. Frida died when she was still young.	T	F

D Read the article again. List all the expressions that show contrasting ideas.

1. (Paragraph 1) _____

2. (Paragraph 2) _____

3. (Paragraph 4) _____ . . ., _____

4. (Paragraph 4) _____ . . ., _____

5. (Paragraph 5) _____

6. (Paragraph 5) _____

7. (Paragraph 6) _____

8. (Paragraph 7) _____

A Skim the blog post about an art project. Circle the correct topic.

a. a controversial art gallery   **b.** a controversial artist   **c.** controversial food

Maria's Homework Troubles

Last week, our art teacher showed us Andy Warhol's screen print of a can of Campbell's soup and asked, "Is it art?" So, the task is to do a project to answer the question. Yikes!

I found out that Warhol produced many different versions of the Campbell's soup can—one with 32 cans, one with 100 cans—all done with the same printing method. In other words, he did not even paint them! He also used the same process to produce other artworks: The *Marilyn Diptych*—a canvas showing Marilyn Monroe's face 50 times using the same photograph colored in slightly different ways; *Eight Elvises*, with the same photo of Elvis Presley in a cowboy costume, reproduced eight times in black and white, and many other celebrities and foods. Also, he called his New York studio "The Factory."

I didn't know what to think, so I tried to find out how he explained his works. I read that he said all we, the public, needed to know about his works was right there in front of us. Eureka! I think that may be the key. My ideas are coming in my next post—watch this space!

B Use Maria's notes and her conclusion to write her next post. Look at your answers to **D** in Lesson D and use the expressions that show contrasting ideas to connect Maria's notes.

1. Warhol seems to say that there's nothing deep in his work; I asked myself if that's true
2. he used images that others had produced; he used them in a creative way to make something very different from the original images
3. Ruskin probably wouldn't have called it art; maybe Warhol was commenting on a culture that values celebrities and wealth
4. he was happy to be part of that culture; he represented celebrities and consumer products *in the same way*: the 32 or 100 Campbell's soup cans and Marilyn's 50 faces all look like they are on sale on a supermarket shelf

As promised, here are my ideas for the project to answer my art teacher's tough question:

_____

_____

_____

_____

_____

_____

_____

In conclusion, then, maybe Warhol was saying that in a society in which success is the ability to buy and own things, everything becomes a product on sale. I think he was using the repetition of images to show that people become things that can be bought and sold, too. So, to me, that sounds like art. What do you think?

C Choose a historical controversy. Write a paragraph (100–150 words) to show the contrasting points.

Review

A Match each word to a word or phrase with a similar meaning.

_____ **1.** controversy

_____ **2.** creative

_____ **3.** display (v)

_____ **4.** exhibition

_____ **5.** gallery

_____ **6.** genius

_____ **7.** inspire

_____ **8.** install (v)

_____ **9.** portray

_____ **10.** unique

a. one-of-a-kind

b. set up (v)

c. disagreement

d. show (v)

e. imaginative

f. presentation

g. showroom

h. extraordinary talent

i. excite

j. represent

B Rewrite the reported speech as direct speech.

1. He said he didn't know what to say.

_____

2. Clare promised she would thank everybody for us.

_____

3. Bill said that he and his friends were going to a restaurant near there.

_____

4. I told her I hadn't called her because I had been working all day that day.

_____

5. Pablo said he couldn't eat fries because he was on a diet.

_____

6. Ana said she thought she had met me before.

_____

C Read the sentences and add commas where they are needed.

1. The man who is waving at us is my father.

2. He lives in Bibury which is a very pretty village with his wife and two daughters.

3. We'll be arriving in Hoboken which I love in about two hours.

4. I found the book that I was looking for in a second-hand bookshop.

5. The people who invited them for dinner are our neighbours.

6. The firefighter who rescued her dog which is called Lulu is my friend.

7. Dunja who is a librarian makes wonderful cakes.

8. Syria which is a country in the Middle East is where Angham is from.

Video Antarctica: While You Were Sleeping

A Read the sentences. Then watch the video and write *T* (true), *F* (false), or *DS* (doesn't say).

_____ **1.** Joseph Michael lives in a city.

_____ **2.** Joseph projected his paintings of icebergs on the outside of a museum.

_____ **3.** The museum funded the installation.

_____ **4.** With the use of digital technology, the project was not much of a challenge.

_____ **5.** As most people will never see an iceberg in real life, Joseph wanted to give them a feeling of what they are like.

_____ **6.** Joseph wants people to go away with a clear idea of what he thinks is going on.

_____ **7.** He wants people to have an emotional reaction to his installation.

_____ **8.** He compared the project to peeling an iceberg and putting the peel onto the building.

B Read the sentences and decide what type of word is missing in each space. Write *N* (noun), *ADJ* (adjective), *P* (preposition), *ADV* (adverb), or *V* (verb) in the spaces in parentheses.

1. We live in these _____ (_____) urbanized places covered in concrete, cars, technology all around us, but we _____ (_____) to go back to those _____ (_____) places.

2. I live in the city, and then I come out _____ (_____) places like this and look for _____ (_____), look for that solitude. It's just a combination of the things I _____ (_____).

3. What I _____ (_____) is combine a mixture of set photography, video, moving image. It tends to be _____ (_____) artwork. I'm passionate _____ (_____) exploration.

4. When I'm _____ (_____) photographs, it's just me and the _____ (_____).

5. So, in terms of what I've created _____ (_____) the museum, it's a very _____ (_____) idea. It's an iceberg and it's in the _____ (_____).

6. You think that it's simple, but it's such a complex _____ (_____).

C Watch the video and complete the sentences in the previous exercise.

D Watch the video and order the steps the team took to complete the installation.

_____ **a.** They created scale models of the museum.

_____ **b.** They created a photographic map of icebergs.

_____ **c.** They projected the icebergs onto the real building.

_____ **d.** They created a scan of the museum.

_____ **e.** They organized the expedition to Antarctica.

_____ **f.** They projected the icebergs onto the scale models.

Getting Around

Lesson **A** Vocabulary and Grammar

A Complete the social media post with the words in the box. Four words require a different form.

| aircraft | commute | destination | distance | explore |
| fuel | journey | launch | passenger | transportation |

While (1) _____ is not the only cause of global warming, we burn a huge amount of

fossil (2) _____ every day to keep people and products moving. The way our society

works at the moment is quickly destroying the Earth, so if we want to have a planet to live on,

we need to (3) _____ ways to greatly reduce all (4) _____ that produce

carbon emissions. People often have a long (5) _____ to work. They travel long

(6) _____ because they can't afford to live near where they work. That needs to change.

An affordable public transportation system that ensures (7) _____ reach their

(8) _____ safely is extremely important. Also, at least for a while, we may have to accept

seeing less of the world and reduce (9) _____ travel. Maybe we should

(10) _____ a campaign to remind people that a great vacation doesn't necessarily

need a flight.

B Circle the correct options.

1. Carbon emissions must *be cut / cut* if we want to stop global warming.
2. You could *be taken / take* the next train.
3. Children must *be accompanied / accompany* by an adult.
4. The journey may *be made / make* on foot.
5. Your bicycle could *be fixed / fix* before four o'clock.

C Complete the sentences using the passive.

1. Everyone must switch off their cell phones.
   Cell phones _____.
2. We might cancel trains.
   Trains _____.
3. Passengers must show valid tickets.
   Valid tickets _____.
4. You can book seats online.
   Seats _____.
5. You can use a credit card.
   A credit card _____.

▲ Traffic jams are common during the commute to and from big cities.

A 🎧 15 Listen to the conversation. Check who changes their mind as a result of the discussion.

☐ Kurt   ☐ both

☐ Rosie   ☐ neither

B 🎧 15 Listen again and circle the correct option to complete each sentence.

1. Rosie has borrowed

    a. Kurt's self-driving car.

    b. Kurt's article.

    c. Kurt's tablet.

2. Kurt

    a. is happy about self-driving cars.

    b. has thought about self-driving cars a lot.

    c. thinks self-driving cars are important.

3. Kurt thinks that we must reduce the number of

    a. car accidents.

    b. people working in the back of a car.

    c. cars.

4. Kurt wants to

    a. use his tablet.

    b. know Rosie's questions.

    c. know if Rosie feels sick when reading.

C Read the sentences and write *T* (true), *F* (false), or *NG* (not given).

_____ **1.** Kurt predicts the contents of the article correctly.

_____ **2.** Kurt agrees that having time to work in a car instead of driving is a good idea.

_____ **3.** Kurt can't read in a moving car without feeling sick.

_____ **4.** Kurt is not interested in car safety.

_____ **5.** Rosie disagrees with Kurt's arguments.

_____ **6.** Kurt and Rosie agree that global warming is an emergency.

_____ **7.** Kurt thinks that self-driving cars take people's attention away from the real question.

_____ **8.** Rosie no longer wants to do school projects.

D 🎧 15 Listen again and complete the sentences with three words in each space. Contractions (like *don't*) are one word.

1. Ah. Let me guess. It says that with self-driving cars, fuel (a) _____ because

    (b) _____ more efficiently, accidents (c) _____

    because computers don't make mistakes, and more work (d) _____ by people

    who will not be busy driving.

2. I'll tell you what I think is (a) _____: they're answers to questions that

    (b) _____.

3. Well, first of all, (a) _____ that people can work (b) _____:

    What kind of work (c) _____ in the back of a car?

4. I think the (a) _____ these *improvements* (b) _____

    instead of the ones that (c) _____.

A Complete the sentences with the words in the box. One word requires a different form.

board	fare	pass	route
terminal	ticket	transfer	travel

1. Buying your _____ on the train is more expensive than buying it online.
2. The _____ has changed, and the bus no longer goes to the airport.
3. Trains are very expensive already, yet _____ are increasing again this year.
4. How are you going to _____ to San Diego?
5. Let people get off the train before you _____ it.
6. Can we go into the _____ and have something to eat? We have time.
7. If you're a commuter, a weekly or monthly _____ is the cheapest option for you.
8. There are no direct trains to the city from here. You'll need to _____ at the next station.

B Circle the correct option in each sentence.

1. Do you know where *has John gone* / *John has gone*?
2. *Are they coming* / *They are coming* by train or by bus?
3. What time *does the concert start* / *the concert starts*?
4. Did you find out who *is Engelbert Humperdinck* / *Engelbert Humperdinck is*?
5. Jim would like to know what *are you doing* / *you are doing* tomorrow.
6. *Did Pedro pass* / *Pedro passed* the exam or not?
7. Can you tell me where *is the movie theater* / *the movie theater is*?
8. Does Patti know why *is Max* / *Max is* late?

C Rewrite the questions as indirect questions using the words given.

1. How much are two tickets to Atlantic City?

   Can you tell me _____?
2. Does this bus stop at 82nd Street?

   Do you know _____?
3. Why do you want to go to Asbury Park?

   I'd like to know _____.
4. Is this a direct train, or do we need to transfer?

   I'm wondering _____.
5. Do we get off at the next stop?

   Does Billy know _____?
6. Is there a coffee shop inside the terminal?

   Would you mind telling me _____?

People run and cycle during Ciclovía in Bogotá, Colombia.

When my grandmother was a kid, streets were places where people could walk and bike and where children could play. They didn't even need **road markings**. She says it was wonderful. Then the age of private cars started: sidewalks were built to move **pedestrians** off the street, playing became dangerous, the noise changed from voices and birds to engines and **horns**, and the air became poisonous. In 2018, researchers in the UK showed the connection between the rise of air pollution and the 25 percent increase in **asthma** deaths since 2008.

Some say that new technologies will soon solve the problems that technology has created. I don't think we can wait for that: the planet is being fried, and we need to stop it now. And we already have the technology we need: the bicycle. Many local authorities, tired of waiting for government laws, have taken action and are encouraging cycling. In my view, not a minute too early.

Since 1976, Bogotá has had an official city government program called *Ciclovía* (Bicycleway): Every Sunday, and on public holidays from 7 a.m. to 2 p.m., some of the main roads in the city are closed to cars and taken over by pedestrians, skaters, cyclists, runners, and entertainers. That must be a lot of fun. As more and more people started biking, the city built a very large **network** of bike lanes connected with a bus system. Many other cities have followed Bogotá's example, even if, sadly, in many of them a Ciclovía is only an annual event.

Between 2007 and 2013, almost 400 miles of bicycle lanes and more than 60 car-free squares were built in New York.

Copenhagen, the capital of Denmark, has a special bike path for cyclists, used by around 5,900 people per hour, every day. Cyclists always get a green light when they ride in and out of the city during rush hour. Also, because biking in some weather conditions can be difficult, there are weather sensors on the traffic lights that detect rain or snow and keep the green light on longer for cyclists. A **countdown** clock also shows cyclists when the light will turn green for them, so they can speed up or slow down to avoid having to stop. How great is that?

Studies show that where car traffic is reduced in favor of bicycles, air quality has improved greatly. Everybody must be in a better mood. Of course, some vehicles, like those used by emergency services, are still needed, and public transport needs a bigger **role** in cities built over steep hills. In my opinion, if you have a good public transport system, school buses for every school, and safe bike lanes, not many people would want to use their car and get stuck in traffic.

A Skim the blog post and circle the best title.

1. My Grandmother's Memories
2. Special Lanes
3. An Old-Fashioned Solution

B Read the blog post. Write the words in bold next to their definitions.

1. _____: someone's or something's purpose in an organization
2. _____: a person who is walking in the street
3. _____: a medical condition that makes breathing difficult
4. _____: paint on the road that identifies lanes, crosswalks, parking spaces, etc.
5. _____: a system of connected parts that communicate with each other
6. _____: the act of counting backward to zero
7. _____: the part of a car that makes a loud noise if you press it

C Read the blog post again and write *T* (true) or *F* (false).

_____ 1. When the writer's grandmother was a child, people did things in the streets they can't do now.

_____ 2. The expression "the planet is being fried" refers to global warming.

_____ 3. On Sunday mornings in Bogotá, you can see shows in some of the main roads.

_____ 4. In Bogotá, buses use the network of cycle lanes.

_____ 5. In New York, the space for cars has been reduced and more has been given to bicycles and pedestrians.

_____ 6. In Copenhagen, "weather sensors" are special officials who stop cyclists when riding is dangerous.

_____ 7. In Copenhagen, a cyclist knows when traffic lights will turn green before they change.

_____ 8. The writer thinks that the ideas discussed in the text should be used in the same way in every city.

D Sometimes the writer clearly shows an opinion. Sometimes an opinion is given as fact. Use different colors to highlight the following:

1. Facts
2. The writer's opinion presented as opinion
3. The writer's opinion presented as fact
4. Other people's opinions

A An impartial text gives only facts. A biased text gives opinions for or against its topic. A text can be openly biased (if opinions are presented as opinions), or covertly biased (when opinions are presented as facts). Read the four versions of the same story and match them with the descriptions.

a. impartial

b. covertly biased for

c. covertly biased against

d. openly biased against

_____ **1.** Residents Prevent Drivers from Going to Work Normally

A few residents of an area in Freehold have made going to work very difficult for a lot of people by putting old and ugly furniture in the streets. They claim they are concerned about vehicles speeding in the area. They had asked the city council to do something, but they were rightly ignored. A driver, with understandable anger, called the police, but when the officers arrived, they shockingly allowed the protest to go on, with the excuse that it was peaceful.

_____ **2.** Concerned Parents Peacefully Protest Against Speeding

Residents of a quiet neighborhood in Freehold, tired of the city council's inaction, have put furniture in the streets to force drivers to slow down. They are rightly concerned about vehicles speeding in their streets, especially near an elementary school. "We have repeatedly asked the city council to look into the problem," said Mary Smith, mother of two. Shockingly, however, the council has ignored the residents' understandable fears that something terrible might happen. An insensitive driver called the police, but when the officers arrived, they allowed the good-humored protest to go on. "It's a peaceful protest," said the police captain with a smile. "It only slows cars down."

_____ **3.** Residents Protest Against Speeding

In what I consider an extreme initiative, residents of a neighborhood in Freehold have put furniture in the streets to force drivers to slow down. While I can understand their concerns about vehicles speeding in their area, I don't think they have the right to make people's journey to work difficult. They said they had asked the city council to do something, but no action was taken. In my opinion, these people should let the council consider their options and allow people like the driver who called the police to go earn their money. When the officers arrived, they allowed the protest to go on. In my view, this was a mistake: What will these people do next? Force everybody to bike?

_____ **4.** Residents Protest Against Speeding

Residents of a quiet neighborhood in Freehold have put furniture in the streets to force drivers to slow down. They are concerned about vehicles speeding in their area, especially near an elementary school. "We have repeatedly asked the city council to look into the problem," said Mary Smith, mother of two, "but they have done nothing. We want them to act before something terrible happens." A driver called the police, but when the officers arrived, they allowed the protest to go on. "It's a peaceful protest," said the police captain. "It only slows cars down."

B Read the openly biased text again. Highlight the expressions that show personal opinion.

C Read the two covertly biased texts again. Underline the parts that show bias and explain how each text does it.

D Read the paragraph about Copenhagen in the blog post in Lesson D again. Rewrite it with a covert negative bias.

A Complete the conversation with the correct form of the words in the box.

> aircraft   commute   distance   fuel   journey

Marc: Have you ever heard of "love miles"?

Yu Yan: No, I haven't. Did Ms. Taylor teach it when I missed class?

Marc: No, it's an expression to talk about (1) _____ we make for love.

Yu Yan: Explain, please!

Marc: It means that even if we try not to harm the environment, sometimes we have to make difficult choices. For example, there are many people who don't live in their native country.

Yu Yan: Do you mean (2) _____?

Marc: No. Those are people who travel from home to work every day. I mean migrants who have relatives in a (3) _____ country. You are from China, right? Do you have family there?

Yu Yan: I do. My parents are there.

Marc: Do you travel there often?

Yu Yan: No, but I would like to. It's bad for the environment because of the jet (4) _____ that (5) _____ burn in the atmosphere, but I miss my parents.

Marc: That's what is meant by "love miles!"

B Complete each sentence with a modal and the passive or active form of the verb.

1. If you are stopped by a police officer while driving, you _____ (show) your identification. If you don't, a ticket _____ (give) to you.

2. Movie tickets _____ (purchase) at the counter. You _____ (buy) them online, too.

3. The test _____ (not / do) last week because of the snowstorm. You _____ (do) it this afternoon.

4. Your bike _____ (steal) if you just leave it here. There's a bike rack over there where you _____ (lock) it up.

C Rewrite the indirect questions as direct questions.

1. Do you know how much a monthly pass is?

   _____

2. Can you tell me whether this bus goes to the train station?

   _____

3. I was wondering whether it would be better to get a taxi.

   _____

4. I'd like to know why Peter is late again.

   _____

A Watch the video and complete the questions Chris Anderson asks.

1. Can you _____ us through this? Because this caught so many people's _____.

2. How did you end up an _____ and president of SpaceX?

3. _____ you super-nerdy as a girl?

4. I still don't really believe this video that we're about to play here. _____ on Earth is _____?

5. So how many _____ can possibly afford the fortune of _____ by space?

6. _____ do you believe SpaceX will land the first _____ on Mars?

B Rewrite the questions Chris Anderson asked in **A** as indirect questions.

1. I wonder _____ this.

2. Can you tell us _____?

3. Do you think _____?

4. I still don't really believe this video that we're about to play here. Can you tell us _____?

5. I'd like to know how _____.

6. Can you tell us _____?

C Look at Chris Anderson's questions in **A** and complete the reported speech.

1. Chris Anderson asked Gwynne Shotwell if she could talk them through that because it

   _____

   _____

2. He asked her _____

   _____

3. He asked her _____

   _____

4. He said that _____

   _____

   He asked her _____

   _____

5. He asked her _____

   _____

6. He asked her _____

   _____

Competition

Lesson A Vocabulary and Grammar

A Complete the sentences with the words in the box. Three words require a different form.

athlete	champion	championship	competitor	conquer
event	failure	league	muscle	professional

1. Sportspeople often have to _____ fears, including the very common fear of _____.
2. The best sports teams compete against each other in the top sports _____.
3. Michael Phelps is the swimming _____ who has won the most Olympic medals in history.
4. For a long time, only non-_____ _____ could compete in the Olympic Games.
5. A good warm-up, especially in cold weather, is very important to avoid _____ injuries.
6. In an official running _____, all _____ must have a number pinned on their vest.
7. Most sports have a world _____ that happens every year.

B Match the sentences to the tag questions.

_____ 1. John doesn't like cats,   **a.** isn't he?

_____ 2. You don't know the answer,   **b.** do you?

_____ 3. He's coming to the party,   **c.** are you?

_____ 4. Markus isn't in the office today,   **d.** wasn't he?

_____ 5. You're not going to wear that T-shirt,   **e.** doesn't she?

_____ 6. Alan got a new job,   **f.** is he?

_____ 7. Risa lives in Tokyo,   **g.** didn't he?

_____ 8. Nicholas was late for class,   **h.** does he?

C Add a tag question to each sentence.

1. That kind of snake is dangerous, _____?
2. Some cleaning products are toxic, _____?
3. He wasn't injured in the accident, _____?
4. You hurt yourself, _____?
5. Many accidents at home can be prevented, _____?
6. He's not leaving for the airport yet, _____?
7. They haven't been having the best luck recently, _____?
8. You stayed up late to watch that show last night, _____?

Lesson B Listening

A 🎧 17 Listen to the conversation and match each sportsperson to their sport.

_____ **1.** Judy Guinness   **a.** long jump

_____ **2.** Luz Long   **b.** marathon running

_____ **3.** Matthew Rees   **c.** fencing

B 🎧 17 Listen again and circle the correct answers.

1. What did Judy Guinness do?

   a. She told Olympic judges that they were wrong.

   b. She managed to avoid hurting her opponent.

   c. She refused one point the judges had given her.

2. What did Luz Long do?

   a. He fouled two jumps.

   b. He helped his opponent.

   c. He jumped beyond the line.

3. What did Matthew Rees do?

   a. He let another runner win the marathon.

   b. He stopped a runner from hurting himself.

   c. He stopped running to support a struggling runner.

▲ Judy Guinness stands in silver position on the podium.

C 🎧 17 Listen again and write the answers to these questions.

1. In which year did the Judy Guinness story happen? _____

2. Where did the Olympics take place that year? _____

3. What was the first name of Judy Guinness' opponent? _____

4. In which year did the Luz Long story happen? _____

5. Where did the Olympics take place that year? _____

6. What was the first name of Luz Long's opponent? _____

7. In which year did the Matthew Rees story happen? _____

8. Where did the marathon he ran take place? _____

9. What is the first name of the other runner mentioned in the story? _____

D Read the sentences and write _T_ (true) or _F_ (false).

_____ **1.** Amy is researching stories of great sportsmanship.

_____ **2.** Jasim is not very interested in Amy's project.

_____ **3.** At first, the judges counted extra points that Judy Guinness hadn't scored.

_____ **4.** If he hadn't helped his opponent, Luz Long might have won the Olympic gold.

_____ **5.** Matthew Rees was in trouble before the last 200 meters.

_____ **6.** "Hats off" to someone means you respect and admire that person.

Lesson C Vocabulary and Grammar

A Complete each sentence with a word from the box.

balance	commitment	communication	leadership
speed	stamina	strength	teamwork

1. I'm not sure that _____ between the team and the coach is very good.

2. The individual players are average, but they keep winning because of their great _____.

3. To compete at a high level, you need _____ and many hours of training every day.

4. Running a marathon requires a lot of _____.

5. Gymnasts needs great _____ to be able to jump and not fall when they land.

6. After that terrible first half, it took the team a lot of _____ of character to win the game.

7. Both teams were angry, but both captains showed great _____, and everybody behaved well.

8. I don't know how someone as tall as Usain Bolt can possibly run at that _____.

B Complete the school principal's award ceremony speech with the words from **A**.

Thank you all very much for coming, and welcome to all the parents here. Today we celebrate yet another district championship title for our school's girls' soccer team. Team, we are very proud of you. Each of you has shown great (1) _____ by never missing one practice, and under your captain's (2) _____, you have proved that (3) _____ matters even more than individual brilliance. (4) _____ within the team is so good that sometimes it looks like they can read each other's minds, doesn't it? It's been a long season that has tested our players' (5) _____, and we all feared the worst when in the final, Sharma, our fantastic goalkeeper, lost her (6) _____ and fell badly on one foot. But that's when all that training paid off: the (7) _____ of her muscles kept the ankle from twisting, she was back in goal in no time, and everybody started breathing again. And then we stopped breathing once more ten minutes later when six—six!—of our players ran at amazing (8) _____, beat the opposition's defense, and scored the winning goal. What a moment that was! So, thank you, team, for making us proud. Please give our wonderful team a round of applause.

C Complete each sentence with a relative pronoun. If two pronouns are possible, write both.

1. That's the player _____ was sent off after five minutes.

2. He scored the point _____ changed everything.

3. She's the girl _____ parents could not attend the ceremony.

4. I like movies _____ tell stories about great sportspeople.

5. Will there ever be an athlete _____ can run faster than Usain Bolt?

6. This is the stadium _____ was built for the Olympic games.

A Champion Who Championed Sport for All

When (1) **their** talent brings them wealth and people's attention, some great athletes use (2) **them** to benefit others.

Dutch soccer player Johan Cruyff is a case in point. He was born in April, 1947 in Amsterdam, (3) **which** is home to the soccer team Ajax. Cruyff, (4) **whose** father died when he was 12, grew up in a poor neighborhood near Ajax's stadium, (5) **where** his mother worked as a cleaner. From an early age, he played soccer in the street with other children. Then, at the age of ten, he joined the Ajax youth team.

Cruyff was noticed by Ajax manager Rinus Michels, (6) **who** had invented a new way of playing, called *Total Soccer*. In Total Soccer, all the players (except the goalkeeper) moved around and played all positions. Cruyff was perfect for (7) **it**, as he had the skills, the speed, and the intelligence to play in any position. Soon, his extraordinary talent and spectacular style became very well known internationally, and in addition to being captain of the Netherlands national team, (8) **he** played for various teams in Europe and the US. He was voted best European soccer player of all time, and second best (after the Brazilian, Pelé) in the world.

When (9) **he** was living in the US with his wife and three children, Cruyff noticed a young boy (10) **who** lived next door and was always alone while other children played outside. (11) **He** had Down syndrome, and he was not accepted by the other children. Cruyff started playing with him, and he noticed that the games and sports that (12) **they** played together were helping the child to develop and find some confidence—to the point that one day the boy just walked up to the place (13) **where** the other children were playing and joined them. From then on, he was part of the group.

This friendship confirmed Cruyff's belief that sports are important for children not only because they make them stronger and healthier, but also because (14) **they** connect children to each other even if (15) **they** come from different cultures and have different levels of ability. However, (16) **he** also knew that not all children have an opportunity to play sports: disabilities, lack of money, or lack of space can all stop children from being active.

So, in 1997, Cruyff started the Johan Cruyff Foundation. It builds small soccer fields—called "Cruyff Courts"—with artificial grass in poor neighborhoods, supports projects for children with disabilities, and brings mobile courts to refugee centers. By the time Cruyff died in March, 2016, his foundation had built over 200 Cruyff Courts all over the world, 33 of (17) **which** were specially designed for children with disabilities. The foundation continues his work and has built many more courts since (18) **his** death.

▼ Ajax's stadium was renamed the Johan Cruyff Arena in 2018.

A Skim the article about Johan Cruyff and check the true sentence.

☐ **1.** Cruyff was the best goalkeeper in the history of European soccer.

☐ **2.** Cruyff created his foundation because a young boy asked him to.

☐ **3.** When he was a child, Cruyff had space to play that a lot of children today don't have.

B Read the article. Then read the sentences and write *T* (true), *F* (false), or *NG* (not given).

_____ **1.** Cruyff's parents supported his passion for soccer.

_____ **2.** Ajax is a soccer team in Amsterdam.

_____ **3.** Cruyff's first team employed his mother as a cleaner.

_____ **4.** Cruyff invented Total Soccer.

_____ **5.** Cruyff's style was very exciting to watch.

_____ **6.** Cruyff used sports to connect with a child with a disability.

_____ **7.** Cruyff didn't like children playing outside his house in the US.

_____ **8.** Cruyff believed that children of different backgrounds must not play together.

_____ **9.** Cruyff died soon after his 69th birthday.

_____ **10.** The Cruyff Foundation works for children who don't have access to sports facilities.

C Look at the pronouns in bold in the text and write who or what they refer to.

1. their   *some great athletes* _____

2. them   _____

3. which   _____

4. whose   _____

5. where   _____

6. who   _____

7. it   _____

8. he   _____

9. he   _____

10. who   _____

11. He   _____

12. they   _____

13. where   _____

14. they   _____

15. they   _____

16. he   _____

17. which   _____

18. his   _____

K 120   2011

Johan Cruyff

Malawi

▲ Cruyff's style of soccer was popular all around the world, as shown in his appearance on this postage stamp from Malawi.

A Read the notes for a blog post about a movie. Then number the events in the order they happened.

A Movie *Just* about Sports? Not Quite

I was recently looking for a sports movie to review for my media class, when by chance I found one that was completely new to me. It's a fantasy story, made in the 1980s, and I loved it. It's called *Field of Dreams*.

It's the story of Ray Kinsella. Ray is a young man. Ray has bought a corn farm in Iowa with Ray's wife and young daughter. Years before, Ray had had a disagreement with Ray's father. The argument was about Shoeless Joe Jackson. Shoeless Joe was a controversial baseball player. Shoeless Joe was already dead at the time. Shoeless Joe was Ray's father's hero. Shoeless Joe had been accused of taking money to lose a game. Ray knew that the accusation had never been proven. Ray had told Ray's father that Ray could not respect a man if the man's hero was dishonest. Ray didn't really mean it. Ray's father had unexpectedly died before Ray could apologize.

Now in trouble with Ray's farm, Ray misses Ray's father so much that, following some strange signs, Ray makes the crazy decision to build a baseball field in part of the farm instead of planting corn everywhere. Ray's need to make peace with Ray's father makes Shoeless Joe's ghost appear. Shoeless Joe is followed by many other famous dead baseball players. The players' ghosts mysteriously come out of the corn field to play in Ray's field. Ray realizes that if the players step out of the playing area and cross the white lines, the players will not be able to get back into the playing area, the players will have to return to the corn field and the players will never come out of the corn field again.

One night, Ray asks Shoeless that, in return for building the baseball field, the players allow Ray to follow the players into the corn field, so Ray can see what's in the corn field. Shoeless tells Ray that Ray can't, and Ray gets upset because Ray thinks that Ray deserves a reward. But when all the players have gone back into the corn field, Ray turns around and sees Ray's father.

_____ **a.** Dead baseball players come out to play on the baseball field.

_____ **b.** Ray and his father have a disagreement about Shoeless Joe Jackson.

_____ **c.** Ray meets his father again.

_____ **d.** Shoeless Joe Jackson is accused of taking money to lose a game.

_____ **e.** Ray builds a baseball field, not knowing it is magic.

_____ **f.** Shoeless Joe Jackson stops Ray from following the players.

_____ **g.** Ray wishes he had apologized to his father before it was too late.

_____ **h.** The accusations against Shoeless Joe Jackson are not proven.

_____ **i.** Shoeless Joe Jackson dies.

_____ **j.** Ray's father dies.

B Read the notes for paragraphs 2–4 and write a summary of the story using personal, possessive and relative pronouns, and other expressions to organize the text and avoid repetitions. Make sure the story is clear.

Review

A Complete the text with the correct form of the words in the box.

> athlete   champion   compete   fail

Pierre de Coubertin, the man who reinvented the ancient Greek Olympic Games at the end of the 19ᵗʰ century, (1) _____ the inclusion of physical education in French schools. He believed sports taught young people that the important thing was to (2) _____, not to win. Sports act as a school for life, in which we learn to keep our self-control when we (3) _____, and we learn from our (4) _____. Team sports teach us that in order to win, we don't just need to be (5) _____, but also cooperative—no team can keep winning with just one superstar (6) _____ who doesn't play with his or her teammates. That's why (7) _____ skills are not enough to be a true (8) _____.

B Read the tag questions and complete the statements.

1. _____ going to the track and field event this weekend, aren't you?
2. _____ like raw fish, does he?
3. _____ perform live really well as a group, can't they?
4. _____ working on Friday night, is he?
5. _____ make a lot of money selling sneakers, will he?
6. _____ think about studying harder for the exam, shouldn't they?

C Complete each sentence with a word from the box and a relative pronoun.

> balance   commitment   communication   leadership
> speed   stamina   strength   teamwork

1. There's the gymnast _____ was able to _____ on one hand.
2. _____ is a skill _____ involves more than being someone's boss.
3. She is the woman _____ showed great _____ by lifting the car.
4. Athletes _____ can run long distances demonstrate incredible _____.
5. Body language is one form of _____ _____ a team uses when they play.
6. _____ is important for a group of people _____ needs to meet a deadline.
7. It was his _____ to the sport _____ made him a champion.
8. _____ is just one factor _____ is important for winning an 800-meter race.

A Read the text, then watch the video and write the missing words.

In the mid-1980s, polio once **paralyzed** (1) _____ than 350,000 children a (2) _____ in more than 125 countries. That amounted to a staggering 40 **cases** an (3) _____. By contrast, so far this year, the last **endemic** countries have reported a total of only (4) _____ cases. Since 1988, more than 2.5 billion children have been **immunized** (5) _____ polio, and an **estimated** 16 million children, (6) _____ otherwise (7) _____ have been paralyzed like me, are (8) _____. Despite this incredible (9) _____, we know that until it's **eradicated**, polio remains a very real (10) _____, especially to children in the poorest communities of the world. It can **reemerge** in some of the (11) _____ remote and dangerous places, and from there, it can **spread**. And so this is my new Ironman: to (12) _____ polio.

B Look at the words in bold in **A** and match them with the definitions.

1. _____: probable, but uncertain
2. _____: come back
3. _____: people with a specific disease
4. _____: where something is very common
5. _____: reach an increasing area
6. _____: made someone or something unable to move
7. _____: given something that protects the body from a specific disease
8. _____: removed forever

C Imagine you are watching the TED Talk with a friend. Read what Minda said and complete your comments with the correct tag question.

1. I was born in Bombay, India, and just before my first birthday, I contracted polio, which left me paralyzed from the hips down.
   Oh, wow. That was terrible, _____?

2. Unable to care for me, my birth mother left me at an orphanage.
   That can't have been easy, _____?

3. Fortunately, I was adopted by an American family, and I moved to Spokane, Washington just shortly after my third birthday.
   That must have been good, _____?

4. As a child, I struggled with my disability.
   You can understand that, _____?

5. I have the humbling knowledge that, had I not been adopted, I most certainly wouldn't be in front of you today.
   She wouldn't be, _____?

Danger

Lesson A Vocabulary and Grammar

A Complete the sentences with the words in the box. One word requires a different form.

| accident | allergy | avoid | harm | illness | injury | reaction | risk | safety | sharp |

1. She had a really scary _____ to an insect bite.
2. You may not like it, but there's no _____ in trying it.
3. The car was badly damaged in the _____ but, amazingly, nobody was hurt.
4. An engineer checked the _____ of all the electrical equipment.
5. I always _____ sitting in the sun with no sunscreen on.
6. Can I have a steak knife, please? This one is not _____ enough.
7. He is in a lot of pain because of an old sports _____ he had a long time ago.
8. Do you have any food _____ I should know about?
9. Pollution is a serious health _____ for people with asthma.
10. She's recovering from a long-term _____.

B Rewrite the sentences as negative questions.

1. That looks like the bus you need to catch. <u>Isn't that the bus you need to catch</u>_____?
2. I'm pretty sure she's Terry's sister. _____?
3. Please listen for a minute. _____?
4. I thought he was allergic to eggs. _____?
5. I think you've had enough cake. _____?
6. I can give you a ride home if you want. _____?

C Complete the conversation with appropriate negative questions using the words given.

Maria: I saw Dolores yesterday.

Hans: Really? (1) _____ still in California? (be)

Maria: No, she came back over a month ago. She went back to her old job.

Hans: (2) _____ she hated it? (say)

Maria: She did, so she did a course to retrain as an IT teacher.

Hans: (3) _____? (help)

Maria: It didn't really. She was only offered short-term jobs to cover for people who are sick.

Hans: (4) _____ better than a job she hates? (be)

Maria: Not really, because she could have been without work for a long time.

Hans: (5) _____ too bad? I'm sure she would have been a great teacher. (be)

Lesson B Listening

A 🎧 19 Listen to the conversation. Check the grandfather's job.

☐ **1.** factory worker

☐ **2.** miner

☐ **3.** doctor in a poor village

B 🎧 19 Listen again and circle the correct options.

1. Kitty wants to record her grandfather
   a. for a school project.
   b. because she wants to help him.
   c. because he asked her to.

2. Grandpa thinks that danger
   a. made people take unnecessary risks.
   b. made people think about safety.
   c. brought people together.

3. Grandpa says that in the village
   a. nobody had much.
   b. it was difficult to find a doctor.
   c. some people were richer than others.

4. "Coal fed our children," means that
   a. mothers mixed coal into food.
   b. a person named Coal fed children.
   c. the money from mining paid for food.

C Read the sentences and write *T* (true) or *F* (false).

_____ **1.** Grandpa could have died at his job every day that he went to work.

_____ **2.** Grandpa's father did the same job as him.

_____ **3.** Grandpa says his job wasn't very different from other jobs.

_____ **4.** Some people took unnecessary risks, so nobody trusted them.

_____ **5.** If somebody in the village needed help, somebody helped.

_____ **6.** An illness in a family could make things very hard.

_____ **7.** Grandpa was happy when everything changed in the village.

_____ **8.** Grandpa thinks that people must choose between their health and earning money.

D 🎧 20 Listen again to this part of Grandpa's interview and write the missing words.

We didn't even (1) _____ about it. I mean, we knew it was (2) _____, but I guess what happened was that the (3) _____ made us feel very close—we had very strong (4) _____. It (5) _____ like any other job, where you (6) _____ meet the other workers at the (7) _____ or the (8) _____ and then go (9) _____. We knew we (10) _____ on each other for our (11) _____: someone taking an unnecessary (12) _____ could get everybody (13) _____, just as someone (14) _____ very fast could (15) _____ lives. So, you (16) _____ everybody, and you made sure everybody (17) _____ you. And every day, when we (18) _____ out, we didn't really think about it, but deep (19) _____ we knew we had (20) _____ another day.

A Complete the text with the correct form of the words in the box.

break   bruise   burn   cut   fracture   injury   scrape   sprain

As one of the school's staff members who has had first-aid training, I see students with small

(1) _____ all the time, especially after a sports event. The most frequent and generally least serious

ones are (2) _____: players get hit by another player, a ball, or another object. Very few students

complain about these, unless they are in a lot of pain and fear it may have caused a (3) _____ that

will need surgery to fix—a (4) _____ in a bone is always a bad thing to have. However, if someone's

elbow hits someone's eyebrow, the result can be a (5) _____. If it's deep, they may need to go to

a hospital, but a band-aid is often enough. I also see plenty of (6) _____, especially after soccer

and basketball games: if somebody falls down, they will rub their knee or elbow on the ground. And I

see plenty of (7) _____, too—twisted ankles are rather common. Luckily, I only see (8) _____

if somebody stays out in the sun for too long without sunscreen, which these days doesn't happen very

often because students are aware of the risks.

B Circle the correct word or phrase to complete each adverbial clause.

1. *As soon as / Before* I saw the smoke, I left the building.
2. Don't forget to lock the door *whenever / ever since* you leave the house.
3. I always take a bath *before / as soon as* I go to bed.
4. *Whenever / After* Marta called an ambulance, she tried to help the injured man.
5. *After / When* you walk in the mountains, you should look out for snakes.
6. The child has been afraid of bees *ever since / when* she was stung by one.

C Complete the adverbial clauses with appropriate time expressions.

1. **A:** Could you give me a hand, please?
   B: _____ I've sent this email. Give me one minute.

2. **A:** When did Jamie arrive at the party?
   B: Five minutes _____ you left. If you'd stayed, you'd have seen him.

3. **A:** How often do you go to the gym?
   B. _____ I can. Some days I'm too busy.

4. **A:** How long are you going to stay here?
   B: _____ they tell us to leave. I want to see the band after the show.

A Crime with No Victim

It is difficult to find a movie that has won as many important awards, including the Oscar for Best Documentary, as *Man on Wire*. This is not surprising, as the documentary has almost everything that a great **heist** movie needs: a great story line, suspense, action, police involvement, and interesting characters planning an impossible crime. The only difference between it and the average heist movie is that nobody suffered as a consequence of the crime and nothing was stolen.

Man on Wire is the true story of Philippe Petit, a French **tightrope** artist, who at the age of 18, saw an article about the plans to build two 104-story-high towers for the World Trade Center in New York City, and became obsessed with the crazy dream of walking between the top of the two **skyscrapers** on a **wire**. Walking on a wire above the ground requires great strength, the ability to control every muscle to keep your balance, and complete concentration. Doing it 1,350 feet above the ground means that the smallest mistake or loss of concentration will kill you. Philippe trained and waited for six years until the Twin Towers were built, and then, with the help of some friends, he did it on August 7th, 1974.

The "heist" required complicated planning. First of all, the Twin Towers were private property, so entering without a **permit** was **trespassing**. Philippe needed to study their structure, so he and two friends said they were journalists writing an article about the towers for an important French magazine about architecture, got access to the towers, and took all the photos they needed. Then they studied the buildings and created the complex design to secure the wire between the top of the two buildings safely.

On the evening of August 6th, two of them went to the North Tower and two to the South Tower with fake IDs, carrying the heavy equipment to the roofs, and they worked all night to install the wire. In the morning, other friends met in the street below, and when Philippe, dressed in black, started walking on the wire a quarter of a mile above the ground, they pointed at him, shouting, "Look!" People looked up: from the street they could not see the wire, so what they saw was a man walking on the clouds—something they were not going to forget. He was up there for 45 minutes and made the crossing eight times.

He was arrested and charged with trespassing and **disorderly conduct**—he did, after all, stop traffic and put himself and others in danger. However, nobody was hurt, nothing was damaged or stolen, and he created wonderful memories for all the **witnesses**. So, he was freed on condition that he did a free show for children in Central Park. His "heist" has been called "the artistic crime of the century."

Philippe Petit performing a tightrope walk

A Read the article. Write the words and phrases in bold next to the definitions.

_____ **1.** a long piece of thin metal, or many pieces twisted together

_____ **2.** very tall buildings

_____ **3.** the act of going onto someone's land or building without permission

_____ **4.** people who see an event happening, especially a crime

_____ **5.** a crime in which a place is entered illegally, and something is stolen from it

_____ **6.** a behavior that threatens the safety of other people

_____ **7.** an official document that allows you to do something

_____ **8.** a long piece of material stretched above the ground that skilled people walk on

B Read the article again and complete the notes.

1. *Man on Wire* is _____.

2. It is like _____.

3. Philippe Petit is _____.

4. For six years, he _____.

5. He lied to _____.

6. The evening of August 6ᵗʰ 1974, he and some friends _____.

7. The morning after, he _____.

8. People in the street _____.

9. The police _____.

10. He was freed _____.

C Complete the summary of the article with suitable words.

    Man on Wire is an unusual (1) _____ that is (2) _____ exciting as a heist movie.
It tells the story of Philippe Petit, a French tightrope artist who (3) _____ six years training and
(4) _____ how to install a wire (5) _____ the Twin Towers of the World Trade Center
in New York City, and to (6) _____ on it. He (7) _____ to get access to the Twin
Towers and, with the (8) _____ of some friends, (9) _____ photos of the structure.
Then, on the evening of August 6th, 1974, he and his friends (10) _____ into the towers
with (11) _____ IDs and (12) _____ the wire during the night. The morning
(13) _____, he walked (14) _____ the roofs of the towers eight (15) _____,
while (16) _____ in the (17) _____ below could (18) _____ believe their
eyes. He was (19) _____, but his action, although (20) _____, was so admired
(21) _____ he was freed on (22) _____ that he performed a (23) _____
show for (24) _____ in Central Park.

A Read the article. Then read the sentences and write *T* (true) or *F* (false).

Sam Springsteen is a firefighter in Jersey City, New Jersey. What is so special about that? Maybe it is not very special, but in 2019, when he passed the test to become a firefighter, it was big news. The reason for this is that he is the youngest son of rock musician Bruce Springsteen and his wife Patti Scialfa, who is also a musician and member of Springsteen's band, the E Street Band.

Bruce Springsteen was born in New Jersey in 1949 into a **blue-collar** family. His father worked first in a factory, then as a security guard, and later had various other jobs, but he was often unemployed. The only salary, very small but at least regular, was brought home by Bruce's mother, who worked as a legal secretary all her life and raised their three children.

Young Bruce made a name for himself locally as a gifted guitar player when he was still in his teens. He played then with some of the musicians whom he went on to play with for most of his life, and who later entered the Rock and Roll Hall of Fame as the E Street Band. Bruce became famous worldwide, writing and singing songs about the lives of young working-class men and women who, like him and his sisters, struggled with the fear that they were not going to have a future.

Of course, those songs brought *him* a future, and in 1984, he started to hold his concerts in stadiums because so many people wanted to see him. His 2016 tour, when he was almost 67 years old, was still in stadiums. However, in spite of the fame and wealth that came with it, he never forgot his roots. He used his money and celebrity status to help organizations involved in assisting people who struggle, and, when he isn't touring, he's known for leading the quiet life of a family man—raising three children on a farm not far from where he grew up—rather than that of a rock and roll star.

That may be why Sam Springsteen's choice made it into the news. He could have had an easy life, with an easy job, enjoying his parents' wealth and connections. Instead, he stayed true to his parents' working-class, community-based values. He chose a job in which he has to run into buildings that other people are running out of, and put his own life in danger to save others. As his mother put it, he is the "family's hero."

blue-collar doing work that requires physical skills, like operating machinery

_____ **1.** Sam Springsteen has very rich and famous parents.

_____ **2.** Bruce Springsteen had very rich and famous parents.

_____ **3.** Bruce Springsteen wrote songs about the community he grew up in.

_____ **4.** Bruce Springsteen usually performs to small numbers of people.

_____ **5.** Bruce Springsteen works with community groups.

_____ **6.** Away from the stage, Bruce Springsteen and Patti Scialfa lead very private lives.

_____ **7.** Sam Springsteen has chosen a career in the same field as his parents.

_____ **8.** Sam Springsteen's parents are embarrassed by their son's career choice.

B Read the text again and write notes in your notebook about the important information in each paragraph.

C Organize your notes and write a summary of the article in your notebook.

A Complete the second sentences so that they mean the same **as the first ones**. Use the words given and any other words you may need.

1. Luckily, the infection was stopped before it caused him serious harm. (harmed, seriously).

   Luckily, the infection was stopped before he _____ by it.

2. There was a car accident, but nobody needed to see a doctor. (injured)

   There was a car accident, but _____.

3. When we tried the new medication on her, we saw a positive **response**. (reacted, positively)

   When we tried the new medication on her, she _____.

4. He is allergic to nuts. (allergy)

   He _____ to nuts.

5. He's in bed with a high temperature. (sick)

   He _____.

6. They decided not to climb the mountain because it was too dangerous. (risky)

   They decided that the mountain _____.

7. I'm allergic to gluten. Will I be OK if I eat this cookie? (safe)

   I'm allergic to gluten. _____ for me to eat this cookie?

8. They discovered the new treatment by chance. (accidental)

   The discovery _____.

B Match the sentence halves.

_____ 1. He had a purple bruise on his arm

_____ 2. She fractured her toe when she

_____ 3. The blood stopped as soon as

_____ 4. I cleaned the scrape before it

_____ 5. She put her hand under cold running water

_____ 6. She sprained her ankle six weeks ago and she

_____ 7. He broke his nose when he

_____ 8. It's a very old injury he got when he

a. hasn't been able to walk since then.

b. they bandaged the cut tightly.

c. half an hour after the ball hit it.

d. fell into the goalpost.

e. immediately after getting burned.

f. dropped a box on it.

g. was a child.

h. could become infected.

C Complete the information with the time expressions.

| after | as soon as | before | until | when |

In the event of an emergency, exit the building _____ you hear the alarm. _____ leaving the building, do not run, and do not use the elevators. Do not collect your belongings _____ heading to the exit—you can get them _____ you are told the building is **safe** to reenter. Please wait patiently in the waiting area _____ the firefighters tell you to go back in.

Video   An Everyday Danger

A Watch the video and write *T* (true) or *F* (false).

_____ **1.** Xaviar is dying from a serious illness.

_____ **2.** He is in danger all the time.

_____ **3.** He is allergic to chicken.

_____ **4.** He is allergic to eggs.

_____ **5.** He can't eat peanut butter.

_____ **6.** Food allergies never change.

_____ **7.** Contact with other children may be dangerous for Xaviar.

_____ **8.** His mother didn't tell him about the allergies because she doesn't want him to be anxious.

B Read the following list of actions. Check the ones Xaviar's mother needs to do.

☐ **1.** Stop Xaviar from coming into contact with other children

☐ **2.** Prepare Xaviar's food every day

☐ **3.** Take Xaviar to the doctor's once a week

☐ **4.** Check the ingredients in foods she didn't prepare

☐ **5.** Test Xaviar's food before he eats it

☐ **6.** Be ready for emergencies

☐ **7.** Make sure Xaviar knows what to do if he has a reaction

☐ **8.** Stop Xaviar from talking to other children

☐ **9.** Try to raise Xaviar so that he's confident

☐ **10.** Make sure Xaviar has a list of his allergies with him

C Read the following list of fears. Check the ones that Xaviar's mother mentions in the video.

☐ **1.** Teachers may not understand food allergies.

☐ **2.** Other children may touch foods Xaviar is allergic to and touch things Xaviar will touch.

☐ **3.** Xaviar may develop new allergies.

☐ **4.** Xaviar may eat foods he knows he can't eat.

☐ **5.** Other people may give Xaviar foods he's allergic to.

☐ **6.** Xaviar may not have a normal life when he grows up.

☐ **7.** She may have done something before Xaviar was born that caused his allergies.

☐ **8.** She doesn't know what the next reaction will be like.

D Do you know anybody who has an allergy? If you do, write a paragraph explaining the things they have to be careful about. If you don't, imagine the life of someone allergic to plastic. Write about 150 words.

Mysteries

Lesson A Vocabulary and Grammar

A Complete the sentences with the words in the box. Three words require a different form.

ancient	civilization	doubt	knowledge	possibility
speculate	suggestion	theory	uncertain	wonder

1. Our _____ of how the brain works is still limited.
2. They made some helpful _____ about how to solve the problem.
3. There are many _____ about what causes food allergies, but that's all they are.
4. Disease may have been a factor in the fall of the Aztec _____ in Mexico.
5. There is a strong _____ that this new treatment will work.
6. This handwritten document is very precious and _____, but nobody knows what it says.
7. It was a difficult decision, and they _____ what to do for a long time.
8. There is no _____ that he stole it because he was caught on camera.
9. Until we know all the facts, we can only _____.
10. The origin of the mysterious object is still _____.

B Complete the conversation with words in the box.

doubt	doubtful	know	knowledge	possible	speculation	suggest	theoretical

Ali: I think I found a new star.

Clara: What, with that telescope? I (1) _____ it.

Ali: Why? You (2) _____ nothing about telescopes or stars.

Clara: I don't need a lot of (3) _____ to (4) _____ that the discovery of a new star is (5) _____ because all the stars that can be seen with much more powerful telescopes already have names.

Ali: Well, anything is (6) _____—maybe a new star was born, and I was the first to see it.

Clara: Maybe there is a (7) _____ possibility, but you'll have to prove it. Until you do, I'm not even sure you can call it (8) _____—sounds more like dreaming to me.

C Circle the correct options.

1. We don't know why he left. He *may be called / may have been called* back to the hospital.
2. She doesn't want to go out. She *could be worried / could have been worried* about the exam.
3. They *may miss / may have missed* the train and that could explain why they're late.
4. He *must forget / must have forgotten*. I'll go call him.
5. She *could be / could have been* allergic to eggs—she's having tests done.
6. They *may go out / may have gone out*, but they left the door unlocked.

Mysteries 73

A 🎧 22 Listen to the podcast and answer the questions.

1. What is an inside job?

    a. work that cannot be done outside a building

    b. a crime in which the criminals are helped by somebody who works for the victim

    c. a crime that only people in the criminal world know about

2. What is an accomplice?

    a. someone who helps a criminal

    b. someone who accomplished something important

    c. someone who only works with a partner

B 🎧 22 Listen again and answer the questions.

_____ **1.** On what date did the robbery take place?

_____ **2.** How many thieves carried out the robbery?

_____ **3.** How many security guards were on duty that day?

_____ **4.** How long did the robbery take?

_____ **5.** How many artworks did the thieves take?

_____ **6.** What is the total value of the stolen artworks?

C Complete the summary of the podcast with one word in each space.

Isabella Stewart Gardner was an art collector. She

(1) _____ a large private museum where her

collection could (2) _____ enjoyed by the public.

The museum was robbed in the year (3) _____,

when (4) _____ thieves dressed as

(5) _____ asked the security guards to let them in

to (6) _____ strange noises. The thieves tied up the

security guards and, in (7) _____ minutes, managed

to steal artworks worth a total of $(8) _____ million.

There are many (9) _____ about who organized the

heist and why, but (10) _____ of the questions have

been answered, so the police can only (11) _____.

(12) _____ has been arrested and

(13) _____ of the artworks have been recovered.

This makes it the world's biggest (14) _____ art theft.

▲ The courtyard at the Isabella Stewart Gardner Museum

Lesson C Vocabulary and Grammar

A Complete the text with the words in the box. Three words require a different form.

character	clue	crime	deduction	detective
evidence	investigation	proof	speculate	theory

In most mystery books and movies, someone breaks the law, and there is one main

(1) _____—a police officer or a (2) _____—who has to find out who

did it. Usually we—the readers or viewers—follow him or her and know only what he or she knows, so

what happened is a mystery for us, too. We (3) _____ about what happened and have

our own (4) _____.

A different type of story was made very popular by the TV series *Columbo*. The hero is Lieutenant

Columbo from the Los Angeles Police Department, and in this show, we see the (5) _____

and who does it at the beginning of each episode. In other words, we know more than Columbo does.

Columbo is always badly dressed, talks too much, and is more friendly and open with the people he is

investigating than detectives in other shows. During the (6) _____, he tells the criminals

about the (7) _____ he finds and the (8) _____ he makes, but that he has

no (9) _____. The criminals think that he is not very smart, and that they are safe. But in

the end, when they least expect it, he shows them a very small mistake that they made and that is

(10) _____ that they did it, so he always catches the bad guy.

B Match the two halves of the sentences, based on the text in the previous exercise.

1. In most mystery stories, we only know
2. In Columbo stories, we know from the beginning
3. What we don't know is
4. Columbo doesn't know
5. Columbo tells the criminals
6. The criminals don't know

a. how Columbo is going to catch the criminal.
b. what he has found out.
c. how smart Columbo is.
d. what the police officer or the detective knows.
e. what we know.
f. who committed the crime.

C Read the text. Underline the subject noun clauses and circle the object noun clauses.

Clue is a popular board game that was created in Britain. A crime has been committed in a large country house in England. The players have to find out who committed the crime, in which room it was committed, and which weapon was used. What you need to play is three sets of cards: six suspects, nine rooms, and six weapons. Three cards, one from each set, are taken out and put in an envelope so nobody has them and nobody can see them—they are the correct answer. There is a complicated set of rules about how the players move on the board and when they can explain their theory about what happened. You also need to make notes about how the other players behave: how they react to a theory gives away clues about which cards they have. The first player who guesses correctly which cards nobody has wins. Sounds difficult? What you need is a little practice!

The Mysteries of Nazca

In the desert of Peru, the Nazca Lines have <u>mystified</u> people for <u>decades</u>. Seen from the ground, they look like <u>random</u> lines scratched into the earth, but from high above, these marks are huge images of birds, fish, and seashells. That's why these <u>patterns</u> were not discovered until the 1930s, when pilots first saw them while flying over the area. In all, there are about 70 different human and animal figures, along with 900 triangles, circles, and lines.

▲ A monkey can be seen in the Nazca Lines of the Peruvian desert.

Researchers believe that the lines are at least 1,500 years old. They know what techniques were used to make them, but what nobody knows is why they were made. And like all unsolved mysteries, this has attracted a lot of speculation.

I think the most unlikely explanation is the one a Swiss writer named Erich von Däniken came up with. In 1968, he wrote that the Nazca lines were designed as a landing place for UFOs by people who received instructions from **extraterrestrials**—a sort of airport for alien spaceships.

The American explorer Paul Kosok had a more <u>plausible</u> theory. In the 1940s, he suggested that the drawings were a map of the movement of the stars and planets and called Nazca "the largest <u>astronomy</u> book in the world." It was an interesting idea, but unfortunately, when later an astronomer tested this theory on a computer, he couldn't find any connection between the lines and the movements of the stars.

Recently, two other scientists, David Johnson and Steve Mabee, have speculated that the lines could be a giant map of the <u>underground</u> water. Given that the area is one of the driest places in the world, finding water would have been <u>vital</u> for the Nazca people. Other scientists are searching for evidence to prove this.

To me, the most interesting theories, which cannot be proven, are connected with art and religion. Since their appearance on Earth, humans seem to have used art to entertain each other, to record events, and to try to communicate with <u>gods</u>. They built temples and statues, so why not use the desert as a huge <u>canvas</u> to draw amazing art that could be seen from the sky? I prefer to think of these lines as the result of some wonderful artists' imagination asking the god of storms for rain in the desert, rather than the request of an engineer from another planet who wanted an airport.

extraterrestrials beings from other planets

A Skim the article and check the correct answer to the question.

Which of these theories about the use of the Nazca lines have been proven?

☐ **1.** They are an airport for UFOs.

☐ **2.** They are a map of the movements of planets.

☐ **3.** They are a map of underground water.

☐ **4.** They are religious drawings.

☐ **5.** None of these

☐ **6.** All of these

B Read the article. Look at the underlined words and match them with the definitions.

1. _____: essential for life

2. _____: looking like it can be believed

3. _____: beings believed to control some part of life on Earth

4. _____: confused somebody due to being impossible to explain

5. _____: the particular ways in which something is organized

6. _____: a piece of cloth that artists paint on

7. _____: the study of the universe

8. _____: time periods of ten years

9. _____: done by chance and not following a plan

10. _____: below the surface of the earth

C Read the sentences and write *T* (true) or *F* (false).

_____ **1.** The Nazca patterns are too big to be identified from the ground.

_____ **2.** Nobody knows how the lines were drawn.

_____ **3.** Nobody knows why the lines were drawn.

_____ **4.** Scientific evidence shows they were planned on another world.

_____ **5.** A researcher found no connection between the lines and astronomy.

_____ **6.** The lines show rivers that existed in the past but not now.

_____ **7.** The writer agrees with Erich von Däniken.

_____ **8.** The writer thinks that Paul Kosok's theory looked like a possible explanation at first.

_____ **9.** The writer gives no opinion about David Johnson and Steve Mabee's theory.

_____ **10.** The writer believes the lines are religious drawings.

D Read the article again and underline the parts that you used to answer questions 7–10 in **C**. Then underline the correct options to complete the summary of the writer's opinion.

The writer (1) *is / isn't* very interested in the Nazca lines, but she (2) *thinks / doesn't think* that they were designed by extraterrestrials. She (3) *thinks / doesn't think* Paul Kosok's theory (4) *looked / didn't look* interesting, but scientists have shown it cannot be proven. She gives (5) *a positive / no* opinion about David Johnson and Steve Mabee's theory, but she (6) *likes / doesn't like* the idea that the lines were made by artists trying to please gods who (7) *could / couldn't* see from above.

Lesson **E** Writing

A Read Pavel's blog post about Stonehenge. Then read the sentences and check the ones that are true.

Pavel's Blog About Things We Will Never Know

The circle of gigantic stones in the southeast of England, known as Stonehenge, is one of the most famous prehistoric monuments in the world. It receives over a million visitors every year. Archaeologists believe that it was started in about 3000 BC, and that it was modified over time. It is not the only surviving prehistoric stone circle in the world, but it is the one with the most complex architecture and the only one with lintels—the stones that are placed horizontally on top of the vertical ones.

Stonehenge is an extraordinary place but, to me, not because of the facts we have, but because of the questions those facts make us ask and that we cannot answer. Every question points to a mystery.

First of all: When somebody draws a very large circle on the ground, they are saying that the place inside is different from the outside. I think that makes it special in a way that, for example, a rectangle does not. But why was it special?

If then they decide to build the circle using gigantic stones that they have to move from very far away (in this case, over 150 miles away), then they are saying that the place really is special, so I have to ask: Why didn't they build it where the stones were? Why wasn't that place good enough? What does this place have that the other doesn't? What can be the reason for the incredible effort to move these huge stones?

And then, if that wasn't special enough, they build another circle inside the first one—that must surely mean something. So, now I wonder: What is even more special about the circle inside the circle? Who is allowed there? Who is not? Is it for especially important people, like kings or religious leaders? Is it for especially bad people, like prisoners or people who have to be punished in some way? And why does the sunlight hit the center of the monument at sunrise on the longest day of the year and at sunset on the shortest day of the year? Is this by chance, or did they plan it?

That's why I love Stonehenge so much: because someone decided it was special for reasons I will never know, made it special, and left us with a mystery that cannot be solved.

1. ☐ There are no other prehistoric stone circles in the world.
2. ☐ There are no other prehistoric stone circles with lintels in the world.
3. ☐ Stonehenge was originally a stone rectangle.
4. ☐ The stones used to build Stonehenge were not originally at that location.
5. ☐ The Stonehenge circle was originally built somewhere else and then moved.
6. ☐ Stonehenge is made of two circles, one inside the other.
7. ☐ Only kings and religious leaders were allowed inside Stonehenge.
8. ☐ The sun marks the center of Stonehenge on the longest and shortest days of the year.

B Read the blog post again. Identify the facts and circle the writer's opinions.

C Use the prompt to write a paragraph summarizing Pavel's opinion about Stonehenge.
Pavel thinks that Stonehenge is an extraordinary place because of _____

D Choose an unsolved mystery from your native country and write a short essay presenting facts and your opinion about it. Write at least three paragraphs and about 250 words.

Review

A Match the words with their meanings.

1. ancient
2. civilization
3. uncertain
4. knowledge
5. possibility
6. speculate
7. suggestion
8. theory
9. wonder

a. human development
b. chance
c. guess
d. think about
e. very old
f. possible explanation
g. information
h. not sure
i. recommendation

B Circle the best modal to complete each sentence.

1. The detective can't find the evidence he collected. He *could* / *must* have lost it.
2. The investigation is over. The police *might* / *must* have found proof.
3. The crime *could* / *must* have happened over the weekend, but we don't know.
4. The main character in the story *may* / *must* have committed the crime, but I don't know yet.

C Change the questions into noun clauses. The first one is done for you.

1. How old is his cat?

   I don't know how old his cat is _____.

2. Who are they?

   Do you know _____?

3. What did he do?

   Please tell me _____.

4. Why did they leave?

   _____ is unknown.

5. Whose bag is this?

   I don't know _____.

Video From Ancient to Modern

A Who controlled ancient Mesopotamia? Watch the video and put the names in order.

a. _____ Assyria and Babylon

b. _____ Persia

c. _____ the Akkadian Empire

d. _____ city-states

B Match the words from the video with their definitions.

1. city-state

2. empire

3. flexible

4. goods

5. palace

6. ruins

7. settlement

8. temple

a. a place where people come to live where not many had lived before

b. large building built for or by rich and important people

c. a city and the area around it with an independent government

d. things that are bought and sold and that can be moved

e. a group of countries controlled by a single person, government, or country

f. the remaining parts of an ancient building or town

g. a name that some religions call a building used for worship

h. able to change or be changed depending on the situation

C Watch the video and circle *T* (true), *F* (false), or *NG* (not given).

1. Western civilization began in Mesopotamia.	T F NG
2. There were human settlements in Mesopotamia more than 6,000 years ago.	T F NG
3. People settled in Mesopotamia from India.	T F NG
4. When the Akkadian Empire fell, the area became Babylon and Assyria.	T F NG
5. The Mesopotamians studied astronomy.	T F NG
6. The Mesopotamians developed the Zodiac.	T F NG
7. Some Mesopotamian kings became rich by selling palaces.	T F NG
8. Writing was originally used by people who worked in trade.	T F NG
9. Speakers of many languages adapted the cuneiform writing for their language.	T F NG
10. The Mesopotamians had written laws.	T F NG

D In your notebook, write about an ancient civilization that was very important in your native country. Explain why and write about 150 words.

Assyrian warriors shown in structural art ▶

Learning

Lesson A Vocabulary and Grammar

A Complete the text with the words in the box. Two words require a different form.

academic	achieve	attend	concentrate	confidence
curriculum	degree	expert	motivation	training

I'm the youngest of four children, and my brothers and sisters had started (1) _____

our local high school years before me. That can give you very powerful (2) _____:

they seemed so grown-up, to me, and I wanted to be like them. Unfortunately, this excitement didn't last

long. Instead of learning, we were just trying to cover the (3) _____. Classes were just a

form of (4) _____ to pass the exams. I struggled to (5) _____. My grades

dropped, and so did my (6) _____, especially after a teacher told my parents I had

no (7) _____ talent, and it was better not to push me to try to (8) _____

more than I could. And then I discovered astronomy, and it all changed. I'm now studying with some of

the world's greatest (9) _____, and I'm finishing my college (10) _____ this

summer!

B Circle the correct options.

1. I wonder what Abraham Lincoln *should / would* have thought of this.
2. You *should / would* have called me instead of doing all that work on your own.
3. She *would / could* have been injured in the accident, but luckily, she wasn't.
4. He *should / would* have put sunscreen on—look how sunburned he is.
5. I *shouldn't / wouldn't* have made pizza if I'd known you hate it.

C Complete the text with the correct form of *should / would / could have* and the verbs in parentheses.

Members of the jury, I'm here to tell you that my client (1) _____ (not / commit)

this crime because she was in Philadelphia that day. She (2) _____ (not / be)

there because she had a meeting to attend here, but her manager made her go to Philadelphia. She

never trusted her manager, and, on the train, she thought she (3) _____ (say)

no to him. However, she didn't because she was sure she (4) _____ (get) in

trouble if she had. She (5) _____ (lie) and said she was sick, but she knew her

manager (6) _____ (find out). But that was her lucky decision, and you will hear

witnesses saying she (7) _____ (not / be) at the crime scene because she was

hundreds of miles away. I will prove to you that this trial (8) _____ (never / start).

Lesson B Listening

A 🔊 24 Listen to the podcast. What is it about?

    a. Accents and why they matter   **b.** Critical thinking and why it matters

B 🔊 24 Listen again and check the correct options.

1. Professor Said thinks that
   - ☐ **a.** Paco's English is not correct.
   - ☐ **b.** people don't speak correctly.
   - ☐ **c.** everybody has an accent.

2. Professor Said thought that
   - ☐ **a.** her relative was not very smart.
   - ☐ **b.** slow talkers are not very smart.
   - ☐ **c.** people from Louisiana are not very smart.

3. Professor Said thinks that
   - ☐ **a.** we need to examine what we believe.
   - ☐ **b.** our beliefs are nearly always wrong.
   - ☐ **c.** we must try to disagree with others.

4. Professor Said thinks that it is important
   - ☐ **a.** to have the right feelings.
   - ☐ **b.** to talk to people we disagree with.
   - ☐ **c.** to win arguments.

C Match the words and expressions.

_____	**1.** put something to the test	**a.**	have
_____	**2.** reason	**b.**	confusion about what something means
_____	**3.** hold	**c.**	supporting argument
_____	**4.** misunderstanding	**d.**	decide the value of something
_____	**5.** evaluate	**e.**	examine something

D Complete the summary of the podcast using the words in the box. Use each word only once.

able	control	effect	evidence	examine	false	hidden
hold	how	little	reason	somebody	test	truth

Critical thinking is a way of thinking by which you (1) _____ your beliefs to make sure you have good (2) _____ for them. We may (3) _____ beliefs that we formed when we were young and knew very (4) _____ about life. We need to (5) _____ our beliefs because important decisions that we make may be based on ideas we don't know we have, but they (6) _____ our lives. If they are (7) _____, they will have negative (8) _____ on our lives. So, we need to ask (9) _____ we know what we know and evaluate arguments and (10) _____. Talking with people we disagree with is very helpful because they show us our (11) _____ beliefs. They may also see things we don't see that we need to evaluate to find the (12) _____. If we do that, we will be (13) _____ to choose beliefs that are our own and not (14) _____ else's.

Lesson C Vocabulary and Grammar

A Complete the first part of the description with the words in the box.

boarding school	campus	continuing education	enroll
gap year	homeschooling	major in	private school

Lawyers in Space is the worst TV show I have ever seen. The first episode starts like a classic rags-to-riches story. As a child, Ben had to help his father on the farm, so his mother provided him with some basic (1) _____. Ben was very bright, so after he got a job at the age of 16, he was able to (2) _____ for evening classes in the department for (3) _____ at the local community college. Then he got a scholarship and was offered a place at the local university to (4) _____ law. He lived on (5) _____, but he was very unhappy. Other students had been to (6) _____, and some even to (7) _____, so he thought everybody was smarter than him. He made friends with an older student, Charlie, who had just come back from his (8) _____ in Australia.

B Circle the correct form of each verb to complete the second part of the description.

What Ben didn't know was that Charlie, whose father was a British lawyer and diplomat, (1) *would / should* cause him trouble. At the age of four, Charlie (2) *will / was going to* move from England to France, where his father (3) *could / was going to* work for the government. Two days before the move, Charlie's father was accused of a crime he had not committed and mysteriously disappeared. Charlie's mother, also a lawyer, sent Charlie to live with family in the US. The separation (4) *is / was* only going to be temporary, as she was sure she (5) *could / would* be able to prove her husband's innocence. What she didn't know was that she (6) *is soon going to / would soon* be arrested, too.

C Complete the final part of the description with the future in the past of the verbs in parentheses.

At first, Charlie's mother's arrest meant that it (1) _____ (take) longer for her to bring her son back. She didn't know that she (2) _____ (spend) ten years in prison. In the meantime, her husband discovered that the proof of his and his wife's innocence was held on the International Space Station. So, he decided that the only way he (3) _____ (be) free was by going there himself. According to his plan, he (4) _____ (train) at a secret location and, with the help of a friend, he (5) _____ (get) on the next mission to the Space Station. However, the government found out, and stopped their plan. That's why as soon as he and Ben got their law degrees, Charlie decided they (6) _____ (become) astronauts and go to the International Space Station themselves. That's when I realized the show was terrible, and I stopped watching it.

1. _____

In 1993, neurologist Oliver Sacks published an article in *The New Yorker* called "To See and Not To See" in which he told the story of a man, Virgil (not his real name), who had lost his eyesight when he was a child, but had gotten it back after an operation 45 years later. The doctors thought the operation had been successful and excitedly waited for the bandages to come off and to see the happiness on Virgil's face. They and Virgil were greatly disappointed, though: Virgil's eyes could see, but his brain could not understand the images it was receiving from his eyes. In other words, the brain had lost the ability to process the data the eyes were sending, and what his eyes saw made no sense to him. This told Sacks that images are not formed in our eyes but in our brain—**i.e.**, the camera doesn't know what it is recording.

2. _____

Sacks's conclusion is helpful in discussing dyslexia. The brain of a dyslexic person seems to process data from the eyes in a way that is different from how a non-dyslexic brain does it. As a result, there are considerable differences between how easily each group can perform the same tasks. The most obvious difference is that many dyslexics struggle with reading, writing, and lists. That is because these tasks are sequential: they depend on the ability to detect and remember the order of letters in words and words in sentences, which a dyslexic brain finds difficult to process.

3. _____

However, dyslexics can accurately identify visual patterns and where the pattern is broken more easily than non-dyslexics. This is what a team of psychologists from the University of Wisconsin-Eau Claire discovered in 2003. They conducted an experiment in which they gave participants a number of images and asked them to pick out the ones that showed impossible things. They found that people with dyslexia were the fastest at the task.

4. _____

Dyslexics can also think in images, visualize 3-D shapes from 2-D drawings, think creatively about ideas that do not seem connected, and find solutions more easily and often better than non-dyslexic people. This explains why dyslexic people excel at visual arts, architecture, math, science, and critical thinking. Although dyslexia was not known at the time, Picasso, Edison, Walt Disney, Agatha Christie, and Einstein, just to give a few examples, were probably dyslexic. They all did terribly in school because of their dyslexia, but then went on to make their mark on the world.

5. _____

For Virgil, however, regaining his sight at 50 might have been too late. Although the operation had fully repaired his eyes, his brain never learned how to process images again, and he almost completely lost his sight again, not long after the operation.

i.e. (Latin, *id est* = that is) formal way to say *in other words*

▼ Dutch artist M.C. Escher created pieces of art that showed impossible situations.

A Skim the article and choose the best title.

1. Two Types of Brain

2. Virgil's Story

3. Advantages and Disadvantages

B Read the article again. Match the headings to the paragraphs.

a. Spot the Nonsense

b. A Sad Conclusion

c. Sequences? No, Thanks!

d. Virgil

e. The Bigger Picture

C Read the sentences and write *T* (true) or *F* (false).

_____ 1. Virgil stayed blind because his brain didn't know what to do with images.

_____ 2. We understand what we see because the brain forms the correct image of it.

_____ 3. If you're dyslexic, it's probably difficult for you to read letters in the correct order.

_____ 4. If you're dyslexic, you'll probably notice mistakes in patterns very quickly.

_____ 5. If you're dyslexic, you probably love making lists of things to remember.

_____ 6. If you're dyslexic, you probably find it easy to visualize things that don't exist yet.

_____ 7. If you're dyslexic, you're probably not very creative.

_____ 8. Dyslexia has been studied for centuries.

D Compare the first paragraph of the article and the text below. Circle the information in the article that is missing in the paragraph below, and underline the differences in vocabulary, spelling, and style. Then check the best practices for essay writing.

    Oliver Sacks published an article in which he told the story of this guy, Virgil, who had become blind at some stage but then had an operation and could see again. The doctors thought the operation had gone well and were hoping that Virgil was going to be happy with not being blind. But they and Virgil were very disappointed: Virgil's eyes could see, but Virgil's brain couldn't understand the stuff it was getting from his eyes. That is, the brain couldn't process the data the eyes were sending, which in practice means that we see with our brain and not with our eyes. Wow.

☐ 1. Use formal language.

☐ 2. If you can, say where your information comes from.

☐ 3. Use contractions.

☐ 4. Use the passive where possible.

☐ 5. Use precise language.

☐ 6. Use colloquial, friendly language.

☐ 7. Give facts and figures where possible.

A Read the essay. Then look at the underlined parts and match them with the best practices they **fail** to follow. Write the numbers. Some parts break more than one rule.

The Unexamined Life Is Not Worth Living

Socrates was an ancient Greek philosopher, (1) <u>and I think he's</u> the father of Western philosophy. (2) <u>There are some theories about when and where he was born</u>, but he died in Athens in 399 BC.

He was the first philosopher to think that (3) <u>philosophy is for finding the truth</u>, and that the most important truth to find (4) <u>is what</u> the *good life* is—(5) <u>that is</u>, the right way to live your life as a good person in society. (6) <u>You recognize you're ignorant and you go from there</u>, examining your beliefs in detail. (7) <u>You find the truth talking to others</u>: (8) <u>they say what they think, and you ask questions to test their belief</u>. If, for example, that belief seems good for the individual, but (9) <u>bad for</u> society, then (10) <u>it's</u> wrong. (11) <u>If you can't find faults</u>, then that belief is probably correct. He invented critical thinking.

This is why he never wrote anything. (12) <u>As he knew he was ignorant</u>, he believed the only thing he had to teach was a method for finding the truth: ask questions until you find answers that (13) <u>can't</u> be wrong. How do we know what we know about him? Through the conversations between him and other people that two of (14) <u>his students wrote down</u>. But then, are those Socrates's words and ideas, or his students'? It (15) <u>doesn't</u> matter; what matters are the ideas and the method, not (16) <u>his name</u>.

a. Use formal language. _____

b. Use the passive where possible. _____

c. Use precise language. _____

d. Give facts where possible. _____

B Read the essay again. Make notes about information that should be added. Do a quick search on the internet to find it.

C Rewrite the essay in your notebook following the best practices for essay writing and include the missing information. Use some of the words and expressions in the box.

be prepared	believed	considered	harm	ignorance	in this case
on that basis	purpose	starting point	test	uncertain	

▼ A statue of Socrates at the Academy of Athens in Greece.

A Complete the sentences with the words in the box. Two words require a different form.

academic	academy	achievement	attendance
concentration	confident	motivate	train

1. You need to improve your _____; you shouldn't have missed class this morning.

2. She couldn't have studied harder, so she was _____ she was going to pass.

3. One of his greatest _____ was opening a youth center.

4. He wanted to be an actor, but he would have had to go to a performing arts _____.

5. This job requires high _____: a mistake can cost lives.

6. She wants to _____ to be a plumber.

7. To be a successful _____, you need to be good at researching and fundraising.

8. I don't like people who are _____ by greed.

B Complete each sentence with a word or phrase from the box.

boarding school	campus	continuing education	enroll
gap year	homeschooling	major in	private school

1. He hated _____ because he missed his classmates.

2. What is it like for children who live at a _____ to be away from their family?

3. He decided to _____ in film studies, but he may not be able to finish the course.

4. Sending your children to a _____ must be very expensive.

5. With so many buildings, it took me some time to find my way around the _____.

6. The film is about a woman who _____ rocket science.

7. She's taking a _____ to travel, and then she may or may not go to college.

8. There are lots of part-time courses for workers in the department of _____.

C Complete the sentences with a future in the past form of the verbs in parentheses.

1. The mother had no idea how she _____ (afford) her children's education.

2. The students hoped that the school play _____ (be) successful.

3. The teachers knew they _____ (have) to help the students prepare.

4. The elderly couple decided they _____ (do) anything with their retirement money.

Video   SOLA Power

A Read the dictionary definition below. Then look at the title of the video and answer the question.

pun wordplay; joke or humorous use of an expression based on the fact that the expression has more than one meaning or that it sounds like another expression

What other expression does the pun in the title refer to?

_____

B Watch the video and match the words with the definitions.

confident	empowerment	initiate	priority
privilege	right	serve	sibling

1. _____: something that people have by law
2. _____: a brother or sister
3. _____: cause something to begin
4. _____: to be of service to
5. _____: an advantage that only some people have, usually because they are rich and/or powerful
6. _____: certain of your abilities
7. _____: something that is very high on a list of important things to do or deal with
8. _____: the process of gaining the ability to control what happens to you

C Complete the sentences with the correct form of words from the box in **B**.

1. Life and personal safety are basic human _____.
2. She comes from a large family and has five _____.
3. He's excellent at his job and he's very _____.
4. Happiness is the number one _____ in my life.
5. She always expects special treatment because she comes from a _____ family.
6. They _____ the conservation program three years ago.
7. She _____ as a city council member for five years until 2019.
8. We work for the _____ of people who have no access to education.

D Watch the video again. Then write a summary to explain what SOLA is doing for girls in Afghanistan. Use some of the words from the box in **B**.

Innovation

Lesson A Vocabulary and Grammar

A Complete the sentences with the words in the box. One word requires a different form.

creativity	device	electronic	habit	invention
outcome	purpose	significant	solution	success

1. Some people develop the bad _____ of constantly checking their phones.
2. It looks nice and expensive, but I don't understand its _____.
3. The 1960s were a time of great _____ in western art.
4. The problem seemed impossible, but we found a _____.
5. The process has started, but we won't know the _____ for a few weeks.
6. You can install this antivirus software on all your _____.
7. It looks like the experiment was a great _____.
8. The *e* in *email* stands for _____.
9. The _____ of the steam engine started the Industrial Revolution in 18ᵗʰ century Britain.
10. Marie Curie won Nobel Prizes for her _____ contributions to two different sciences.

B Complete the sentences with the correct form of the words in the box.

create	invent	solve	succeed

A bad invention can (1) _____ more problems than it

(2) _____. When plastic was (3) _____,

many everyday problems were (4) _____, but it also

(5) _____ in becoming a major source of pollution.

C Change each sentence into the future using the words given. There may be more than one possible answer.

1. She can swim very well.
   I'm sure _____ well after a few more lessons.
2. You need to see a dentist now.
   _____ soon, even if you don't want to.
3. The principal can see you now.
   Wait here. _____ in ten minutes.
4. He needs to study for the exam tomorrow.
   _____ hard over the next few weeks.
5. I can't give you an answer now.
   _____ until I've talked to my parents.

A 🎧 26 Listen to the conversation. Who invented the telephone?

1. Alexander Graham Bell

2. Antonio Meucci

3. Elisha Gray

4. We don't know for sure.

B 🎧 26 Read the sentences and write *T* (true) or *F* (false). Then listen again and check your answers.

_____ **1.** A patent is a document that says that you own an invention.

_____ **2.** It is possible that Bell based his telephone on other people's work.

_____ **3.** Meucci was a Cuban inventor who emigrated to Italy first.

_____ **4.** Meucci wanted to build a telephone to help his sick wife.

_____ **5.** Meucci applied for a one-year patent because he didn't want to pay for a longer patent.

_____ **6.** Meucci and Bell didn't know each other.

_____ **7.** Western Union treated Meucci very well.

_____ **8.** Bell died before he could defend himself from the accusations.

C Complete the text about the invention of the telephone. There is more than one correct answer for each space, but do not use the same word more than once.

On March 10th 1876, just three days after he had received his (1) _____ for it, Alexander Graham Bell used a (2) _____ to call his assistant in another room and said, "Mr Watson, come here. I want to see you." However, he may have been using a (3) _____ that he had not (4) _____ himself. It is certain that part of it was based on Elisha Gray's design, which Bell had seen. However, Bell only used that part for the model in that experiment. After that, he did not use it for commercial purposes.

What happened with Antonio Meucci's design is less clear. It looks like Bell's telephone (5) _____ based on the model that Meucci had (6) _____, which Bell was familiar with. However, as Meucci was too (7) _____ to pay for a long patent, Bell had the (8) _____ to develop Meucci's design. In (9) _____, the US Congress stated that if Meucci had been able to pay for a (10) _____ patent, Bell would not have been allowed to apply for one himself. Meucci (11) _____ as poor as he was born and Bell became a very (12) _____ man.

Lesson C Vocabulary and Grammar

A Complete each sentence with a word in the box.

ambitious	beneficial	curious	enthusiastic
essential	practical	smart	versatile

1. It's _____ that we get an answer before we do anything else.

2. Rice is one of the most _____ foods I know. I can make at least 30 dishes with it.

3. Most medicines are _____ only if you take them for a short time.

4. I don't think going there three times this week will be very _____.

5. She's very _____ about the project and puts a lot of energy into it.

6. He was so _____ that he was prepared to break rules to become rich and powerful.

7. He was always very _____ about nature, so he became a biologist.

8. She's incredibly _____ and always gets good grades.

B Circle the correct options to complete the conversations.

1. **A:** Do you have any plans for tonight?

   B: Yes, I *'m going* / *'ll go* to the basketball game with Jamal. His dad gave him two tickets.

2. **A:** What time is your bus?

   B: It *will leave* / *leaves* the station at five o'clock, so it should be here in 20 minutes.

3. **A:** Can you wait for me here? I need to get some cash from the ATM around the corner.

   B: I *'ll come* / *'m coming* with you, if you don't mind. I've just realized I need cash, too.

4. **A:** I *'m probably going to make* / *probably make* pizza tonight. Why don't you come over?

   B: Oh, great! I think I *do* / *will*, thanks! Can I bring anything?

5. **A:** What *are you going to* / *do you* get Mario for his birthday?

   B: I don't know yet. I *'m going* / *go* shopping on Saturday morning. Do you want to come?

6. **A:** Don't worry, Mom, I promise I *'m texting* / *'ll text* you when I get there.

   B: Don't forget! I just know I *won't be able to* / *don't* sleep until I know you're OK.

C Complete the conversation with the correct form of the verbs in parentheses. There is no verb for one of the spaces because you need to give a short answer.

Ilya: I (1) _____ (go) to the football game tonight. (2) _____ (you, want) to come?

Amy: Great idea—I think I (3) _____. What time?

Ilya: The game (4) _____ (start) at seven o'clock, but if we want good seats

we (5) _____ (need) to be there at least an hour earlier.

Amy: OK. No, wait! I forgot! I (6) _____ (babysit) my brother tonight! I promised my

parents! It's their anniversary today, and they (7) _____ (go out) for dinner.

Ilya: Can't you get anyone else to do it?

Amy: I (8) _____ (try) Grandma. Let me call her.

Landscapes, Illustrations, and Humor

William Heath Robinson was a British cartoonist and illustrator who was born in London in 1872 into a family of artists: his father was an illustrator, and both his older brothers also became illustrators before him. He studied art at Islington Art School and then at the Royal Academy to become a landscape painter, but he soon realized that he wouldn't have been able to earn enough money to pay the bills. So, he put aside his landscape painting ambitions and started working as a book illustrator.

Until that time, printed illustrations could only be simple because the technique used for printing them, called woodblock printing, would have required too much time and work to reproduce complicated drawings. Additionally, they could only be printed in black and white. However, recent innovations allowed illustrations to go straight to print without going through the woodblock process, which meant that much more complex artworks could be reproduced in books. At the same time, more innovations made printing in color also possible.

Heath Robinson took full advantage of the new technology to show what he could do. In the year 1900, he created beautiful, complex pen and ink drawings to illustrate a collection of poems by Edgar Allan Poe, and in 1902, he produced wonderful watercolor images for a full-color edition of *Don Quixote* by the Spanish author Miguel de Cervantes.

Things seemed to be going well: 1902 is also the year in which he wrote and illustrated his first book of children's stories, *The Adventures of Uncle Lubin*, and the following year, he married Josephine Latey. However, they had just had their first daughter when the publisher with which Robinson had a large contract went **bankrupt**, so he had to find another source of income to feed his family.

That's when he started publishing the cartoons he is best known for: illustrations of enormously

▲ *The Multimovement Tabby Silencer*

complicated machines built to achieve ridiculously simple outcomes, which he used to make gentle fun of people's confidence in technological solutions to solve problems that did not need technology. His crazy inventions use the steam power of pots, the heat of candles, and complex systems of wheels, ropes, **parachutes**, and balloons to do things like throw water at a noisy cat. It's not just the images of the inventions that are crazy—they also have names like *The Multimovement **Tabby** Silencer*. His huge and complex machine for making holes in blocks of cheese involves a giant fork and four men to operate it.

He was so successful that, in the UK at that time, "Heath Robinson" was the term used to refer to unnecessarily complicated machines. His serious work has remained very influential with illustrators, and his humor lives on in Wallace, the inventor of crazy machines in the stop-motion animation movies from British director Nick Park about the adventures of Wallace and his much smarter dog: Gromit.

bankrupt unable to pay what you owe and having to close your business
parachute a large piece of special cloth and long ropes used to slow down a person's fall after jumping from an airplane
tabby a house cat with dark marks on gray or brown fur

A Skim the article and circle *T* (true) or *F* (false).

1. Heath Robinson was an inventor.   T   F
2. Heath Robinson was an engineer.   T   F

B Read the article. Then read the sentences and write *T* (true) or *F* (false).

_____ **1.** Illustrating books was Heath Robinson's first choice of career.

_____ **2.** He was a very skilled artist.

_____ **3.** He was not very interested in the details of the printing process.

_____ **4.** He illustrated Poe's poems with black and white drawings.

_____ **5.** He published more than one children's book.

_____ **6.** He didn't like unnecessary technology.

_____ **7.** His work was only appreciated after his death.

_____ **8.** Recent animated movies carry on Heath Robinson's ideas.

C Answer the questions in full sentences.

1. Why did Heath Robinson study art?

_____

_____

2. Why did he become a book illustrator?

_____

_____

3. Why was he able to produce complex linework illustrations?

_____

_____

4. Why was he able to produce watercolor illustrations?

_____

_____

5. Why did he start creating cartoons?

_____

_____

6. What was *The Multimovement Tabby Silencer* for?

_____

_____

D Read the article again and underline all the phrases that describe purpose.

A Read the blog post about the first science fiction story. Then match the sentence halves.

Mary Shelley's *Frankenstein* is considered the novel that started both the horror and the science fiction genres and asks essential questions about science, its responsibilities, and the long-term effects of inventions.

It tells the story of a brilliant scientist, Victor Frankenstein, whose mother dies when she is young, so he decides that the purpose of his research will be to fight death and give back life to the dead. He steals bodies from graveyards to build a "creature" and invents a machine to make it come to life. The experiment is successful, but Frankenstein is scared by the monstrous appearance of his creation, and abandons the man he has given life to. However, first of all, Victor never thinks about the effects his actions may have on others in general and on the creature in particular; and secondly, he fails to take responsibility and manage the results of his blind ambition.

At first, the creature tries to fit in, learns to speak by observing and listening to others, and teaches himself to read, but people reject him, and he ends up with no human connections. He finds Victor's notes with the details of his own monstrous birth, so he meets his "father" to explain to him what horror life is when your body has experienced death before, when you don't know *what* you are, when people run away when they see you, and as a result, all you feel is anger. He wants Victor to accept his responsibility, stop hating him, and make him a female companion to share his life with. When Victor fails to do any of these, many innocent people die before the creature and his "father" die, too.

_____ **1.** Victor's purpose is to   **a.** make his creature come to life.

_____ **2.** Victor wants a device for   **b.** fight death.

_____ **3.** Victor uses body parts to   **c.** building a creature.

_____ **4.** For Victor, body parts are for   **d.** bringing people back from death.

_____ **5.** Victor builds a machine to   **e.** accept responsibility

_____ **6.** The creature wants Victor to   **f.** build a creature.

B Read the sentences and write *T* (true) or *F* (false).

_____ **1.** Victor was extremely upset by his mother's death.

_____ **2.** Victor thinks about how the relatives of the people whose bodies he steals might feel.

_____ **3.** Victor thinks about whether the body parts will give memories to the creature.

_____ **4.** Victor thinks about how the creature will feel when it comes to life.

_____ **5.** Victor thinks about how society will respond to the creature.

_____ **6.** Victor wanted to do something good for humanity.

_____ **7.** Victor takes care of the creature when it comes to life.

_____ **8.** The story asks if anything that is possible should be made.

C Think of an innovation that had both good and bad effects and write an essay about it. Describe its purpose and how it works, what the effects were, and what scientists should have thought of but did not.

Review

A Complete the sentences with *have to* or *be able to*. Then state whether each one describes an *ability* or a *necessity*.

_____ *necessity* _____ **1.** He might _____ *have to* _____ get creative if he wants to find a solution.

_____ **2.** You will _____ turn off all electronic devices before we take off.

_____ **3.** Clara won't _____ invent something for that purpose because she doesn't know how.

_____ **4.** He will _____ quit his bad habits in order to be successful.

_____ **5.** She will _____ discover something significant if she continues her research.

B Complete the sentences using the verbs in parentheses so that they explain what will happen in the future.

1. The store _____ (open) at eight o'clock.

2. Wait! Zara _____ (go) with you to collect the money.

3. The flight _____ (depart) at noon, so we should check in at ten o'clock.

4. I'm _____ (babysit) my niece this evening.

5. He _____ (purchase) tickets as soon as they go on sale.

6. He _____ (play) in a tournament this weekend, so he can't meet us.

C Complete the text with the words in the box.

ambitious	beneficial	curious	enthusiastic
essential	practical	smart	versatile

I have never been particularly (1) _____ about science fiction, but after watching a movie called *Arrival*, I've become (2) _____ and have started reading and watching sci-fi. I realized that sci-fi is not really about the future. I mean, some of it is like that, and all it does is show the (3) _____ (or sometimes damaging) effects of (4) _____ scientific discoveries in people's lives. But as a story genre, sci-fi is very (5) _____, so it can be much more than that. It can ask questions like, "What if ...?" and use a story about robots to explore the relationships between humans and machines. Some authors and directors with (6) _____ purposes have produced some (7) _____ works that use sci-fi to ask not simply important, but (8) _____ questions about what it means to be human, and I like that a lot.

Video   Why You Should Make Useless Things

A Watch the video. Simone uses these words. Put them in the correct columns.

| ambitious | anxiety | embarrassed | expectation | fail | fear |
| feel stupid | nervous | pressure | problem | self-conscious | severe |

Nouns	Verbs	Adjectives

B Match the words from **A** to the definitions.

1. _____: worry caused by responsibilities

2. _____: worried about what people think of you

3. _____: not succeed

4. _____: the unpleasant emotion of being frightened

5. _____: a thing or situation that needs to be solved

6. _____: having a strong desire to be successful, powerful, or rich

7. _____: feel not very intelligent

8. _____: the uncomfortable feeling of worry about something that may happen

9. _____: causing great pain, difficulty, worry, or damage

10. _____: worried and anxious

11. _____: feeling ashamed or shy

12. _____: the feeling or belief that something will or should happen

C Look at the list of words in **A**. Which do you think are causes? Which are effects?

D Simone uses *would* to talk about habitual actions in the past and to talk about future actions in the past. Read these extracts from her talk. Circle the habitual actions in the past and underline the future in the past.

1. I came up with a setup that would guarantee success 100 percent of the time. With my setup, it would be nearly impossible to fail. And that was that instead of trying to succeed, I was going to try to build things that would fail.

2. But one thing I'm actually really nervous about is my hands shaking. I remember when I was a kid, giving presentations in school, I would have my notes on a piece of paper, and I would put a notebook behind the paper so that people wouldn't be able to see the paper quivering.

Spelling Rules for Verbs Ending in -s and -es

1. Add -s to most verbs.	like-like**s** sit-sit**s**
2. Add -es to verbs that end in -ch, -s, -sh, -x, or -z.	catch-catch**es** miss-miss**es** wash-wash**es** mix-mix**es** buzz-buzz**es**
3. Change the -y to -i and add -es when the base form ends in a consonant + -y.	cry-cr**ies** carry-carr**ies**
4. Do not change the -y when the base form ends in a vowel + -y.	pay-pay**s** stay-stay**s**
5. Some verbs are irregular in the third-person singular -s form of the simple present.	be-**is** go-**goes** do-**does** have-**has**

Spelling Rules for Verbs Ending in -ing

1. Add -ing to the base form of most verbs.	eat-eat**ing** do-do**ing** speak-speak**ing** carry-carry**ing**
2. When the verb ends in a consonant + -e, drop the -e and add -ing.	ride-rid**ing** write-writ**ing**
3. For one-syllable verbs that end in a consonant + a vowel + a consonant (CVC), double the final consonant and add -ing. Do not double the final consonant for verbs that end in CVC when the final consonant is -w, -x, or -y.	stop-stop**ping** sit-sit**ting** show-show**ing** fix-fix**ing** stay-stay**ing**
4. For two-syllable verbs that end in CVC and have stress on the first syllable, add -ing. Do not double the final consonant. For two-syllable verbs that end in CVC and have stress on the last syllable, double the final consonant and add -ing.	ENter-enter**ing** LISTen-listen**ing** beGIN-begin**ning** ocCUR-occur**ring**

Spelling Rules for Verbs Ending in -ed

1. Add -ed to the base form of most verbs that end in a consonant.	start-start**ed** talk-talk**ed**
2. Add -d if the base form of the verb ends in -e.	dance-danc**ed** live-liv**ed**
3. When the base form of the verb ends in a consonant + -y, change the -y to -i and add -ed. Do not change the -y to -i when the verb ends in a vowel + -y.	cry-cr**ied** worry-worr**ied** stay-stay**ed**
4. For one-syllable verbs that end in a consonant + a vowel + a consonant (CVC), double the final consonant and add -ed. Do not double the final consonant of verbs that end in -w, -x, or -y.	stop-stop**ped** rob-rob**bed** follow-follow**ed** fix-fix**ed** play-play**ed**
5. For two-syllable verbs that end in CVC and have stress on the first syllable, add -ed. Do not double the final consonant. For two-syllable verbs that end in CVC and have stress on the last syllable, double the final consonant and add -ed.	ORder-order**ed** HAPpen-happen**ed** ocCUR-occur**red** preFER-prefer**red**

Spelling Rules for Comparative and Superlative Forms

	Adjective/Adverb	Comparative	Superlative
1. Add -er or -est to one-syllable adjectives and adverbs.	tall fast	tall**er** fast**er**	tall**est** fast**est**
2. Add -r or -st to adjectives that end in -e.	nice	nice**r**	nice**st**
3. Change the -y to -i and add -er or -est to two-syllable adjectives and adverbs that end in -y.	easy happy	eas**ier** happ**ier**	eas**iest** the happ**iest**
4. Double the final consonant and add -er or -est to one-syllable adjectives or adverbs that end in a consonant + a vowel + a consonant (CVC).	big hot	big**ger** hot**ter**	big**gest** hot**test**

Common Irregular Verbs

Base Form	Simple Past	Past Participle	Base Form	Simple Past	Past Participle
begin	began	begun	make	made	made
break	broke	broken	meet	met	met
bring	brought	brought	pay	paid	paid
buy	bought	bought	put	put	put
come	came	come	read	read	read
do	did	done	ride	rode	ridden
drink	drank	drunk	run	ran	run
drive	drove	driven	say	said	said
eat	ate	eaten	see	saw	seen
feel	felt	felt	send	sent	sent
get	got	gotten	sit	sat	sat
give	gave	given	sleep	slept	slept
go	went	gone	speak	spoke	spoken
have	had	had	swim	swam	swum
hear	heard	heard	take	took	taken
hurt	hurt	hurt	tell	told	told
know	knew	known	think	thought	thought
leave	left	left	throw	threw	thrown
let	let	let	understand	understood	understood
lose	lost	lost	write	wrote	written

Phrasal Verbs (Separable) and Their Meanings

*Don't forget to **turn off** the oven before you leave the house.*
*Don't forget to **turn** the oven **off** before you leave the house.*

Phrasal Verb	Meaning	Example Sentence
blow up	cause something to explode	*The workers **blew** the bridge **up**.*
bring back	return	*She **brought** the shirt **back** to the store.*
bring up	1. raise from childhood 2. introduce a topic to discuss	*1. My grandmother **brought** me **up**.* *2. Don't **bring up** that subject.*
call back	return a telephone call	*I **called** Rajil **back** but there was no answer.*
call off	cancel	*They **called** the wedding **off** after their fight.*
cheer up	make someone feel happier	*Her visit to the hospital **cheered** the patients **up**.*
clear up	clarify, explain	*She **cleared** the problem **up**.*
do over	do again	*His teacher asked him to **do** the essay **over**.*
figure out	solve, understand	*The student **figured** the problem **out**.*
fill in	complete information	***Fill in** the answers on the test.*
fill out	complete an application or form	*I had to **fill** many forms **out** at the doctor's office.*
find out	learn, uncover	*Did you **find** anything **out** about the new plans?*
give away	offer something freely	*They are **giving** prizes **away** at the store.*
give back	return	*The boy **gave** the pen **back** to the teacher.*
give up	stop doing	*I **gave up** sugar last year. Will you **give** it **up**?*
help out	aid, support someone	*I often **help** my older neighbors **out**.*
lay off	dismiss workers from their jobs	*My company **laid** 200 workers **off** last year.*
leave on	allow a machine to continue working	*I **left** the lights **on** all night.*
let in	allow someone to enter	*She opened a window to **let** some fresh air **in**.*
look over	examine	*We **looked** the contract **over** before signing it.*
make up	say something untrue or fictional (a story, a lie)	*The child **made** the story **up**. It wasn't true at all.*
pay back	return money, repay a loan	*I **paid** my friend **back**. I owed him $10.*
pick up	1. get someone or something 2. lift	*1. He **picked up** his date at her house.* *2. I **picked** the ball **up** and threw it.*
put off	delay, postpone	*Don't **put** your homework **off** until tomorrow.*
put out	1. take outside 2. extinguish	*1. He **put** the trash **out**.* *2. Firefighters **put out** the fire.*
set up	1. arrange 2. start something	*1. She **set** the tables **up** for the party.* *2. They **set up** the project.*
shut off	stop something from working	*Can you **shut** the water **off**?*
sort out	make sense of something	*We have to **sort** this problem **out**.*
straighten up	make neat and orderly	*I **straightened** the messy living room **up**.*
take back	own again	*He **took** the tools that he loaned me **back**.*
take off	remove	*She **took off** her hat and gloves.*
take out	remove	*I **take** the trash **out** on Mondays.*
talk over	discuss a topic until it is understood	*Let's **talk** this plan **over** before we do anything.*
think over	reflect, ponder	*She **thought** the job offer **over** carefully.*
throw away/ throw out	get rid of something, discard	*He **threw** the old newspapers **away**.* *I **threw out** the old milk in the fridge.*
try on	put on clothing to see if it fits	*He **tried** the shoes **on** but didn't buy them.*
turn down	refuse	*His manager **turned** his proposal **down**.*
turn off	stop something from working	*Can you **turn** the TV **off**, please?*
turn on	switch on, operate	*I **turned** the lights **on** in the dark room.*
turn up	increase the volume	***Turn** the radio **up** so we can hear the news.*
wake up	make someone stop sleeping	*The noise **woke** the baby **up**.*
write down	write on paper	*I **wrote** the information **down**.*